SpringerBriefs in Law

SpringerBriefs present concise summaries of cutting-edge research and practical applications across a wide spectrum of fields. Featuring compact volumes of 50 to 125 pages, the series covers a range of content from professional to academic. Typical topics might include: • A timely report of state-of-the art analytical techniques • A bridge between new research results, as published in journal articles, and a contextual literature review • A snapshot of a hot or emerging topic • A presentation of core concepts that students must understand in order to make independent contributions SpringerBriefs in Law showcase emerging theory, empirical research, and practical application in Law from a global author community. SpringerBriefs are characterized by fast, global electronic dissemination, standard publishing contracts, standardized manuscript preparation and formatting guidelines, and expedited production schedules

Saskia Stucki

One Rights: Human and Animal Rights in the Anthropocene

 Springer

Saskia Stucki
Max Planck Institute for Comparative Public Law
and International Law
Heidelberg, Germany

Open Access funding provided by Max Planck Society and Max Planck Institute for Comparative Public Law and International Law

ISSN 2192-855X ISSN 2192-8568 (electronic)
SpringerBriefs in Law
ISBN 978-3-031-19203-6 ISBN 978-3-031-19201-2 (eBook)
https://doi.org/10.1007/978-3-031-19201-2

© The Author(s) 2023. This book is an open access publication.
Open Access This book is licensed under the terms of the Creative Commons Attribution 4.0 International License (http://creativecommons.org/licenses/by/4.0/), which permits use, sharing, adaptation, distribution and reproduction in any medium or format, as long as you give appropriate credit to the original author(s) and the source, provide a link to the Creative Commons license and indicate if changes were made.

The images or other third party material in this book are included in the book's Creative Commons license, unless indicated otherwise in a credit line to the material. If material is not included in the book's Creative Commons license and your intended use is not permitted by statutory regulation or exceeds the permitted use, you will need to obtain permission directly from the copyright holder.

The use of general descriptive names, registered names, trademarks, service marks, etc. in this publication does not imply, even in the absence of a specific statement, that such names are exempt from the relevant protective laws and regulations and therefore free for general use.

The publisher, the authors, and the editors are safe to assume that the advice and information in this book are believed to be true and accurate at the date of publication. Neither the publisher nor the authors or the editors give a warranty, expressed or implied, with respect to the material contained herein or for any errors or omissions that may have been made. The publisher remains neutral with regard to jurisdictional claims in published maps and institutional affiliations.

This Springer imprint is published by the registered company Springer Nature Switzerland AG
The registered company address is: Gewerbestrasse 11, 6330 Cham, Switzerland

*For Derek & Banjo –
my human & animal companions*

and for the unnamed cat
whose suicide so brutally embodied
the unbearable banality of evil.
May you rest in peace now.

Preface

This book is the third part of my postdoctoral research project *Trilogy on a Legal Theory of Animal Rights*, which was generously funded by the Swiss National Science Foundation (2018–2020). The first part of the trilogy, entitled *Towards a Theory of Legal Animal Rights: Simple and Fundamental Rights*, was published in the Oxford Journal of Legal Studies (2020). The second part, entitled *Animal Warfare Law and the Need for an Animal Law of Peace: A Comparative Reconstruction*, is forthcoming in the American Journal of Comparative Law (2023). This book is the final piece of the trilogy. It was (re)written during the ongoing Covid-19 pandemic, which has acutely spotlighted the need to integrate legal concern for human, animal, and planetary health under a holistic One Health approach. This book introduces the novel One Rights approach as a normative response to the increasingly delicate interdependence of human and nonhuman animals and their shared environments.

This book has been a long time in the making, and it is also a well-travelled book. Since its inception in Switzerland in 2015, bits and pieces of the book have gestated and matured in different parts of the world, most notably at the Max Planck Institute for Comparative Public Law and International Law in Heidelberg, Germany, and the Harvard Animal Law and Policy Program in Cambridge, USA. My sincerest gratitude is owed to Anne Peters, Kristen Stilt, and Chris Green for providing me with two hospitable, intellectually curious and conducive, open and supportive academic homes for bringing this book to fruition. I further thank the numerous colleagues who have provided critical feedback on book fragments along the way. Special thanks are owed to Sergio Dellavalle and Raffael Fasel for reading the final book manuscript and giving enormously helpful feedback. I further thank the anonymous reviewers and Brigitte Reschke at Springer for their encouragement and support in publishing this book.

Lastly, my deepest gratitude goes to my family—my parents, my husband, my dog—for their unconditional love, trust, and support. I would not be who and where I am without them.

Heidelberg, Germany   Saskia Stucki

Contents

1 **Animal Rights: A New (Non)Human Rights Revolution?** 1
  1.1 Animal Rights as New Human Rights........................ 2
    1.1.1 What Are Animal Rights?........................... 2
    1.1.2 What Are New Human Rights?........................ 3
    1.1.3 Are Animal Rights New Human Rights?............... 4
  1.2 ... or the End of (Old) Human Rights?..................... 7
  1.3 Something Old and Something New: One Rights 9
  1.4 Approach and Structure of the Book 10
  References 12

2 **Naturalistic Conceptions of Human and Animal Rights: From Human Exceptionalism to Transspecies Universalism** 17
  2.1 Setting the Stage for the 'Theater of Human Law' 17
  2.2 Who Is the 'Human' of Human Rights?...................... 19
    2.2.1 The 'Biological Human' and the 'Essential Human' 19
    2.2.2 The 'Exceptional Human' and the 'Typical Human' 21
  2.3 Exceptionalist Conceptions of Human Rights and the Decline of Old Humanism 22
    2.3.1 Overview 22
    2.3.2 Programmatic Exclusivity 23
    2.3.3 Problems of Exceptionalist Accounts 25
    2.3.4 Against Human Rights Exceptionalism 31
  2.4 Non-Exceptionalist Conceptions of Human Rights and the Rise of New Humanism 34
    2.4.1 Overview 34
    2.4.2 Incidental Exclusivity and Inherent Transspecies Inclusivity 36
    2.4.3 Human Rights Universalism Unbound 39
  References 42

3 Political Conceptions of Human and Animal Rights: Principled and Prudential Reasons ... 49
3.1 Human Rights Denaturalized: Constructing Rights on Practical Grounds ... 49
3.2 The Principled Argument: Human Rights Are Good for Animals ... 52
3.2.1 Human Rights as (Shared) Normative Resource against (Shared) Experiences of Injustice ... 53
3.2.2 Discursive and Rhetorical Function ... 56
3.2.3 Institutional and Universalizing Function ... 58
3.2.4 Aspirational and Transformative Function ... 60
3.3 ... and Animal Rights Are Good for Humans: The Prudential Argument ... 62
3.3.1 Antagonistic and Synergistic Assumptions ... 63
3.3.2 Interconnections Between (Human and Animal) Rights-Generative Phenomena of Social Injustice ... 65
3.3.3 The Environmental Nexus Between Human and Animal Rights ... 76
References ... 81

4 One Rights: Indivisibility and Interdependence of Human and Animal Rights ... 91
4.1 Synthesis: Naturalistic and Political Justifications of Human and Animal Rights ... 91
4.2 Human and Animal Rights as One Rights ... 94
4.2.1 Defining One Rights ... 94
4.2.2 (Some) Human Rights Are Animal Rights ... 95
4.2.3 ... and (Human and Nonhuman) Animal Rights Are (Post-)Human Rights ... 97
4.3 One Rights as Holistic (Post-)Human Rights Paradigm for the Anthropocene ... 99
References ... 102

Chapter 1
Animal Rights: A New (Non)Human Rights Revolution?

> Rights are subject to evolution, if not revolution: both the transformation of currently recognized rights and the introduction of new rights altogether. *Schulz and Raman (2020), p. 6.*

Animal rights is an idea whose time has come.[1] This book looks at animal rights through the lens—and as a phenomenon—of new human rights.[2] It revisits a question once famously asked by the philosopher Paola Cavalieri: are human rights *human*?[3] In other words, can and should animals have some of the same fundamental rights that have traditionally been reserved for humans in the guise of 'human rights'?

Not long ago, the very notion of *human* rights for *nonhuman* animals[4] was easily dismissed as nonsensical.[5] After all, human rights are considered to be 'literally the rights that one has simply because one is a human being'.[6] On the other hand, Christopher Stone reminded us that throughout legal history, each extension of rights to some new group has been 'a bit unthinkable'.[7] When Olympe de Gouges (1791) and Mary Wollstonecraft (1792) first proclaimed the rights of woman in the wake of the 18th century's declarations of the rights of man, the bold proposition that human

---

[1] See Stucki (2020), p. 560 (noting that 'we may presently be witnessing a new generation of legal rights in the making—legal animal rights, simple and fundamental').

[2] On new human rights, see generally von Arnauld et al. (2020); Brysk and Stohl (2017); Bob (2009).

[3] Cavalieri (2005).

[4] Nonhuman animals will hereinafter be referred to as 'animals' and human animals as 'humans'. Furthermore, when speaking of 'animals', what I primarily mean is *sentient* animals.

[5] See e.g. Schulz and Raman (2020), p. 148 (noting that the 'notion that nonhuman animals may be awarded rights is one that many human animals have a hard time taking seriously'); Jowitt (2016), p. 72 (noting that 'it might seem counter-intuitive to be speaking of "human rights" ... for subjects who are, unequivocally, not human. One might consider it axiomatic that human rights apply exclusively to humans').

[6] Donnelly (2013), p. 10.

[7] Stone (1972), p. 453.

rights might also be women's rights was met with much the same incredulity and ridicule as animal rights are today.[8] Indeed, Thomas Taylor (1792) responded to Wollstonecraft's *A Vindication of the Rights of Woman* with the satire *A Vindication of the Rights of Brutes*, likening the case for women's rights to the case for animal rights—of course intended as a *reductio ad absurdum*. Over two centuries later, we can affirmatively state that women's rights *are* human rights,[9] and we may ask in more earnest: are animal rights the next frontier of human rights?

1.1 Animal Rights as New Human Rights...

1.1.1 What Are Animal Rights?

Animal rights are moral and/or legal rights that protect certain aspects of an animal's existence, well-being, intrinsic value, integrity, or other interests.[10] The term 'animal rights' tends to be used differently in theory, practice, and common parlance.[11] In a *broad* sense, it often serves as an umbrella term that covers any kind of (even marginal) protections for animals. For example, *simple* animal rights are the weak and oftentimes odd legal rights that animals may be said to have based on existing animal welfare legislation, such as a right to be slaughtered with prior stunning or a right of chicks to be killed by fast-acting methods, such as homogenisation or gassing.[12] More commonly, however, the notion of animal rights is distinguished from animal welfare law, and conceived as a temporal successor thereof and as a substantive progression therefrom.[13] In a *narrow* sense, then, the term 'animal rights' is typically reserved for a distinctive and more robust kind of normative protection in the form of basic rights, such as the right to life, liberty, and bodily integrity. These *fundamental* animal rights are strong legal rights along the lines of human rights that protect fundamental interests and are not easily overridden by countervailing considerations.[14]

---

[8] Hunt (2007), p. 18, reminds us that 'We should not forget the restrictions placed on rights by eighteenth-century men'.

[9] But see MacKinnon (2006).

[10] For an overview, see Stucki and Kurki (2020).

[11] On the different, broad and narrow senses of animal rights, see Francione and Charlton (2017), p. 25; Kymlicka and Donaldson (2018), p. 320; on the distinction between simple and fundamental animal rights, see Stucki (2020), p. 551f.

[12] Stucki (2020), p. 549.

[13] See Corte Constitucional del Ecuador, Final Judgment No. 253-20-JH/22 ('Estrellita Monkey' case) of 27 January 2022, para 77 (noting that 'the recognition of animals as subjects of rights constitutes the most recent phase in the development of their legal protection, which is based on the recognition of animals as living beings with an intrinsic value that makes them holders of rights'); see also Stucki (2023).

[14] See Stucki (2020), p. 552.

1.1 Animal Rights as New Human Rights...

This book, like most of animal rights theory, is concerned with fundamental animal rights. In this sense, the idea of animal rights is about 'universal basic rights for animals' in virtue of their sentience or 'selfhood'[15]—as it were, fundamental rights that animals have *simply in virtue of being animals*. This dominant understanding echoes that of human rights—the fundamental rights that humans are said to have simply in virtue of being human—and connotes what might be cumbersomely called 'human rights-like animal rights'. Even though animal rights theory has from its inception gravitated towards the natural rights and human rights tradition,[16] contemporary animal rights discourse has taken a more explicit human rights turn. There is now a growing trend to frame animal rights in the language of human rights, and to assert human rights claims on behalf of animals. As a result, animal rights are today considered among an eclectic group of new human rights candidates.[17]

1.1.2 What Are New Human Rights?

New human rights—or claims to such—are novel (contested) rights that seek to enlarge the 'protective umbrella of human rights' beyond the currently accepted catalogue of rights in order to address an extant protective gap or new protective need.[18] New human rights discourses are a constant companion to the established human rights order. This is because human rights, by their very nature, are subject to evolution and revolution; they carry in them the permanent possibility of generating new human rights or extending old human rights to new right-holders.[19] For example, women and children were once new human rights-holders, and today, the right to a healthy environment may be considered one of the newest human rights.[20] Human rights are not static, but rather, in a perpetual state of 'evolutionary flux'[21] and in ongoing need of extension, refinement, and revision.[22] It is this

---

[15] Donaldson and Kymlicka (2011), p. 19ff, 31.

[16] See notably Salt (1892); for an overview of the historical affinity between animal and human rights, see Fasel (2019), chapter 1.

[17] On animal rights as new human rights, see Pietrzykowski (2020); Schulz and Raman (2020), p. 148ff.

[18] von der Decken and Koch (2020), p. 7.

[19] See Schulz and Raman (2020), p. 37 (human rights '"contain the seeds for their own expansion." Sometimes that expansion builds upon current rights in an evolutionary way; other times it reflects the designation of a rights revolution, an expansion of the category of rights holders to a new set of people or new entities').

[20] The human right to a healthy environment was recognized by UN Human Rights Council Resolution 48/13 (8 October 2021) and UN General Assembly Resolution A/RES/76/300 (1 August 2022); on the 'environmental rights revolution' see Boyd (2012).

[21] Alston (1984), p. 616.

[22] Winston (2007), p. 286.

inherent dynamism that enables human rights to respond to changing social, political, ethical, or environmental needs and challenges, and therefore to meet the 'problems that people face in a modern-day world.'[23]

The present era is often referred to as the Anthropocene—the new human-dominated geological epoch in which humankind has become a central force in shaping the global environment, and in which the destructive and escalating impacts of human activities on planet Earth are becoming evermore manifest.[24] In the Anthropocene era, humanity is confronted with a number of new existential risks. These stem from a cluster of interrelated environmental and health crises such as anthropogenic climate change, biodiversity loss, and zoonotic diseases—all of which are intimately linked to our destructive and exploitative relationship with animals and the wider natural world.[25] Contemporary 'Anthropocene problems'[26] are profoundly changing the 'safe operating space'[27] for human rights, and may give rise to new (non)human rights at the human-animal-environment interface.[28] It is in this specific historical context that animal rights as new human rights articulations have started to flourish—fuelled not only by an evolving sense of animal justice, but perhaps more so by an acute awareness of ecological pressures.

1.1.3 Are Animal Rights New Human Rights?

At present, animal rights are new human rights *claims* and as such 'merely candidates for legal recognition'.[29] Broadly speaking, we can distinguish three stages in the 'birth process' of a new human right: from its intellectual inception (the idea phase), to its gradual reception and consolidation in legal and political arenas (the emergence phase), to its eventual legal recognition and codification (the recognition phase).[30] Animal rights are currently located in between the first and second stage of this 'lengthy period of gestation'.[31]

---

[23] von der Decken and Koch (2020), p. 20; Alston (1984), p. 607ff.

[24] On the Anthropocene, see Crutzen and Stoermer (2000); Crutzen (2002); Kotzé (2019).

[25] See generally Sebo (2022).

[26] Purdy (2015), p. 230.

[27] On the notion of a 'safe operating space' within the planetary boundaries framework, see Rockström et al. (2009).

[28] See e.g. Chapron et al. (2019).

[29] von der Decken and Koch (2020), p. 8.

[30] See von der Decken and Koch (2020), p. 7ff; Hannum (2016), p. 410 (the 'imagining, proclamation and eventual codification' of new human rights).

[31] Alston (1979), p. 38 (noting that the process of recognizing a new human right is a lengthy one and involves, inter alia, 'the perception and articulation of a need, the mobilization of support ... and widespread acceptance of both the validity of the need and the responsibility of another party for its satisfaction').

New human rights start out as (oftentimes fringe) discursive articulations by intellectual and political 'norm entrepreneurs' expressing a need to develop existing human rights law.[32] In animal rights discourse, we can clearly discern a human rights turn—a rising trend to articulate and integrate animal rights in the language, concepts, and frameworks of human rights. In animal rights *theory*, a growing body of scholarship casts animal rights as a 'necessary dialectical derivation'[33] or 'logical extension of the doctrine of human rights',[34] and explores the continuities and interconnections between human and animal rights.[35] Conversely, the idea of animal rights is gradually permeating human rights theory,[36] where the 'universal rights of animals' are starting to be considered as a possible 'fourth generation of human rights'.[37] In animal rights *practice*, we can observe a push to have animals' fundamental or human rights legally recognized through legislative or judicial means. For example, a citizens' initiative in the Swiss Canton of Basel-Stadt demanded a constitutional amendment recognizing the fundamental rights of nonhuman primates (which was, however, rejected at the ballot box in 2022).[38] Others have attempted to invoke before courts human rights on behalf of captive animals, such as the right to a fair trial,[39] the prohibition of slavery,[40] or—such is the litigation strategy of the US-based Nonhuman Rights Project—the right of *habeas corpus*.[41] These activities are typical for the first, *idea phase* of new human rights: scholars engage in fleshing out the conceptual foundations and contours of animal rights, while strategic litigation takes first steps to attain human rights for animals in practice.[42] Overall, the once

---

[32] von der Decken and Koch (2020), p. 9.

[33] Cavalieri (2001), p. 143.

[34] Donaldson and Kymlicka (2011), p. 44; Goodkin (1987), p. 260 (viewing animal rights as 'logical progression in the evolution of natural rights theories' which also gave rise to modern human rights theory).

[35] See Cochrane (2013) (viewing human and animal rights as 'part of the same normative enterprise' and making a case for their reconceptualization as 'sentient rights'); Fasel (2019); Peters (2016, 2018); Kymlicka (2018); Gearty (2009); Abbey (2017); Pocar (1992).

[36] See e.g. Douzinas (2000), p. 184ff; Edmundson (2012), p. 153ff; Fellmeth (2016), p. 51ff.

[37] Vincent (2010), p. 147.

[38] See Fasel (2023); in a similar vein, the Finnish Animal Rights Law Society proposes to constitutionally recognize fundamental rights of animals. See https://www.elaintenvuoro.fi/english/.

[39] *Balluch v Austria* App no 26180/08 (ECtHR, 4 May 2008) and *Stibbe v Austria* App no 26188/08 (ECtHR, 6 May 2008). The ECtHR rejected the application for incompatibility *ratione personae*.

[40] *Tilikum v Sea World* 842 F Supp 2d 1259 (S.D. Cal. 2012) (the case was dismissed for lack of subject matter jurisdiction. The court held that the prohibition of slavery applies only to human beings, or persons, but not to orcas, or non-persons).

[41] See, notably, *Tommy v Lavery* NY App Div 4 December 2014, Case No 518336 (rejecting a 'rights paradigm for animals' and determining that 'a chimpanzee is not a "person" entitled to the rights and protections afforded by the writ of habeas corpus'); but see New York Court of Appeals, *Tommy v Lavery* and *Kiko v Presti*, decision of 8 May 2018, motion no 2018-268, concurring opinion Judge Fahey (stating that the question whether an animal can be entitled to release from confinement through a writ of habeas corpus will have to be addressed eventually).

[42] See generally von der Decken and Koch (2020), p. 9.

quixotic idea of extending human rights to animals is gaining wider traction in the political and legal sphere.[43]

Moreover, marking the beginning of the next developmental phase, there is a nascent but growing global animal rights *case law*. Over the past decade, some pioneering courts have embarked on a path of judicial recognition of fundamental animal rights, arriving at them either through a dynamic-extensive interpretation of constitutional (human) rights or via a rights-based interpretation of animal welfare law. Most notably, courts in Argentina[44] and Colombia[45] have extended the fundamental right to *habeas corpus*, along with the underlying right to liberty, to captive animals. In another *habeas corpus* proceeding, the Constitutional Court of Ecuador has recognized a range of basic animal rights as part of the rights of nature.[46] Meanwhile, the Supreme Court of India and Indian High Courts have developed a remarkable case law recognizing and fleshing out the fundamental rights of animals, such as the right to life, dignity, and freedom from torture[47]—or the fundamental right of birds 'to fly in the sky'.[48] The Islamabad High Court has also affirmed a range of fundamental animal rights, and further underscored their nexus with human rights and the 'interdependence of living beings'.[49] Lastly, albeit more tentatively, the Swiss Federal Supreme Court has confirmed the legal possibility of fundamental

---

[43] See Sparks et al. (2020), p. 149f (noting that the 'once quixotic idea of animal rights has . . . turned into a viable legal possibility').

[44] Tercer Juzgado de Garantías de Mendoza 3 November 2016, Expte Nro P-72.254/15 (the judge held that great apes are nonhuman legal persons who possess inherent fundamental rights, such as the inalienable right to live in their habitat, to be born free, and preserve their freedom); this landmark decision was preceded by an *obiter dictum* in Cámara Federal de Casación Penal Buenos Aires 18 December 2014, SAIJ NV9953, para 2 (expressing the view that nonhuman animals are right-holders and ought to be recognized as legal subjects).

[45] Corte Suprema de Justicia 26 July 2017, AHC4806-2017 (MP: Luis Armando Tolosa Villabona) (the judge held that the constitutional right of habeas corpus, which serves to ensure the 'supralegal' guarantee of liberty of the person, can be extended to animals in order to safeguard their respective right to liberty); this ruling was later reversed by the Constitutional Court of Colombia 23 January 2020, Expediente T-6.480.577—Sentencia SU-016/20 (MP: Luis Guillermo Guerrero Pérez), with a noteworthy dissenting opinion by Judge Diana Fajardo Rivera.

[46] Corte Constitucional del Ecuador, Final Judgment No. 253-20-JH/22 ('Estrellita Monkey' case) of 27 January 2022.

[47] See Kerala High Court 6 June 2000, AIR 2000 KER 340 ('If humans are entitled to fundamental rights, why not animals?', para 13); Supreme Court of India 7 May 2014, civil appeal no 5387 of 2014 (deriving a range of animal rights from the Prevention of Cruelty to Animals Act and, by reading them in the light of the Constitution, elevating those statutory rights to the status of fundamental rights).

[48] Delhi High Court 15 May 2015, CRL MC no 2051/2015, paras 3 and 5; Gujarat High Court, *Abdulkadar vs State*, judgment of 12 May 2011, SCR.A/1635/2010.

[49] Islamabad High Court 21 May 2020, W.P. No.1155/2019, paras 59-60 (noting that human rights are natural rights and have a 'nexus with "life"', which makes them available to other living beings. On this basis, the court spelled out a range of natural animal rights, notably the right to live in an environment that meets the behavioural, social and physiological needs of an animal; the right not to be treated in a manner that subjects an animal to unnecessary pain and suffering; and the right not to be tortured or unnecessarily killed); for a discussion of this judgment, see Stucki and Sparks (2020).

animal rights in principle.⁵⁰ Suchlike (as yet still isolated) acts of judicial recognition of animal rights correspond with the early stages of the second, *emergence phase* of new human rights. This stage is characterized by the occurrence of legal activities that are more immediately relevant to the formation of rights, such as courts corroborating the idea of extending fundamental or human rights to animals.⁵¹

Overall, recent developments in theory and practice suggest that legal animal rights are on the horizon, and that fundamental animal rights may be emerging as a new generation of (non)human rights.⁵² We may thus be at the onset of the next, and perhaps most profound, human rights revolution—a *nonhuman rights revolution*: the extension of old human rights to a new class of nonhuman right-holders.

However, animal rights have yet to progress into the final developmental stage of new human rights: legal recognition and codification. Until such wider institutional, political, and legal validation occurs, they remain contested claims or 'wannabe rights'.⁵³ Indeed, among the potpourri of new human rights claims, animal rights are particularly controversial, and contestation and opposition to them perhaps strongest.

1.2 ... or the End of (Old) Human Rights?

As new human rights claims, animal rights are met with strong resistance, if not ridicule or hostility—especially by human rights scholars.⁵⁴ For one thing, the ongoing expansion and proliferation of human rights has generally given cause for concern.⁵⁵ Critical voices warn against such human rights inflation, as it risks undermining the currency, legitimacy, and universality of human rights.⁵⁶ These

---

⁵⁰ Swiss Federal Supreme Court, judgment of 16 September 2020, 1C_105/2019 (confirming the legal validity of a citizens' initiative on primate rights).

⁵¹ See generally von der Decken and Koch (2020), p. 10.

⁵² See also Stucki (2020), p. 533, 560.

⁵³ Hannum (2019), p. 61 (noting that these rights 'should perhaps be called "wannabe" rights, rights whose legitimacy has not been confirmed ... However, mere wishing or proclamation does not create law'); Susi (2020), p. 30 (noting that theoretically articulated new human rights claims move to the next 'stage of contestation from the political establishment and academia').

⁵⁴ See Schulz and Raman (2020), p. 148f (noting that 'Among the most sceptical are human rights advocates ... This indifference or maybe even hostility toward animal rights is ironic, given that many in the animal rights movement either began their careers as human rights activists or took their inspiration from the struggle for human rights').

⁵⁵ On the phenomenon and critiques of human rights proliferation, see generally Alston (1984); Hannum (2019); Tasioulas (2019); Wellman (1999).

⁵⁶ See e.g. Ignatieff (2001), p. 90 (warning that 'rights inflation – the tendency to define anything desirable as a right – ends up eroding the legitimacy of a defensible core of rights'); Hannum (2016), p. 413, 438 ('Human rights are on the verge of becoming a victim of their own success'); Sumner (1987), p. 15 (noting that the 'proliferation of rights claims has devalued rights by eroding their argumentative power').

concerns may appear even more acute with regard to animal rights, considering the sheer number—billions—of potentially entitled animals and the ensuing exponential growth of new human rights-holders and conflicts.[57] Moreover, human rights are already under pressure. In practice, they are undermined by widespread and persistent violations, illiberal backlashes, and an implementation or theory-practice gap.[58] In theory, human rights are an 'essentially contestable concept'[59] that suffers from remarkable foundational uncertainty[60] and are the target of penetrating critiques and challenges.[61] As one commentator has put it, 'Virtually everything encompassed by the notion of "human rights" is the subject of controversy',[62] and as a recent review of human rights theory has concluded, there is a 'diversity of positions ... with no prevailing philosophical view even on fundamental issues like what a human right is'.[63]

Amidst the plethora of problems, one seemingly banal assumption has remained relatively uncontested and operative in most of human rights discourse: that human rights are *human*, i.e., rights held by human beings simply in virtue of their humanity.[64] In this respect, animal rights obviously differ from other new human rights claims in that they aim at a rights expansion *not within but beyond* the human species. Animal rights thus challenge a (perhaps *the*) core axiom of human rights, which may be perceived as a further corrosive trend undermining the viability of human rights. Indeed, against the gloomy backdrop of talk of an 'endtimes of human rights'[65] or a 'post-human rights era',[66] the very idea of taking the 'human' out of human rights[67] and introducing some form of dehumanized,[68] post- or nonhuman

---

[57] In this vein Glendon (1991), p. xi (cautioning that a 'rapidly expanding catalog of rights'—extending to animals and trees—would problematically multiply the sites of collision and risk 'trivializing core democratic values').

[58] Against this backdrop, the result of promoting new human rights 'may be simply to expand the number of rights that are routinely ignored'. Hannum (2019), p. 79.

[59] Griffin (2001), p. 307.

[60] See e.g. Sen (2004), p. 315f (noting that the idea of human rights is seen by many as 'foundationally dubious' and met with 'intellectual scepticism about its conceptual soundness'); Hoffmann (2006), p. 404 (noting that the foundations of human rights are commonly 'only hazily assumed, rather than clearly articulated').

[61] For a discussion of different human rights critiques, see O'Connell (2018); Dembour (2017); Chandler (2016).

[62] Brown (1999), p. 103.

[63] Cruft et al. (2015), p. 4.

[64] See Isiksel (2016), pp. 295–297.

[65] Hopgood (2013).

[66] Wuerth (2017).

[67] See e.g. Lafont (2016).

[68] On the 'dehumanization of human rights'—the process of articulating claims of non-humans 'with concepts, language, and standards borrowed from human rights discourse'—in the context of corporate human rights, see generally Isiksel (2016) (noting, inter alia, that 'human rights are in the process of being appropriated to protect transnational corporations.' Ibid., p. 297); Grear (2007) (critically interrogating the 'corporate colonisation of human rights').

rights might be feared to herald the end of human rights. As Costas Douzinas has summarized these sentiments, 'to question human rights is to side with the inhuman, the anti-human and the evil.'[69]

This book addresses two sets of objections against animal rights in particular: *philosophical* or *conceptual* and *political* or *practical* ones. The first group of concerns relates to the conceptual nature of human rights, which one might say is ill-suited to accommodate animals, because it is intrinsically linked to humanity. Any attempt to insert the nonhuman would be incompatible with, and lead to a collapse of, the very concept of human rights. The second group of objections concerns the practical undesirability of extending human rights to animals. It is often assumed that animal rights are bad for human rights and will lead to harmful consequences, such as levelling down the normative status of (non-paradigmatic) humans.[70] For both types of objections, *opposition to animal rights* is considered a necessary position *in defence of human rights*.[71]

This book seeks to defend animal rights against both the conceptual objection (which maintains that only humans can, and animals cannot, have human rights) and the practical objection (which maintains that only humans should, and animals should not, have human rights). It argues that the inclusion of animals under the human rights paradigm is justified on both philosophical and practical grounds; that is, it is conceptually sound and politically warranted for both principled and prudential reasons. In other words, this book seeks to show that human rights need not be predicated on the exclusion of animals, and that tending to animal rights may ultimately help save human rights.

1.3 Something Old and Something New: One Rights

In a nutshell, this book submits that (some) human rights can and should be extended to animals, and advocates the recognition of animal rights as new human rights. It argues that there are compelling conceptual, principled, and prudential reasons for modernizing and expanding the human rights paradigm anew, and for including animals in its protective ambit. Ultimately, this book advances a holistic understanding of human and animal rights as part of the same family of fundamental rights: One Rights, indivisible and interdependent.

The novel term 'One Rights' is proposed here as a normative companion to the scientific One Health approach.[72] One Rights encapsulates the union of (old) human

---

[69] Douzinas (2000), p. 8.
[70] On this concern (and its refutation), see generally Wills (2020).
[71] See Kymlicka (2018), p. 777 (observing a 'marked trend in the past decade to reassert species hierarchy within the theory and practice of human rights' in an effort to preserve human rights).
[72] On One Health, see Zinsstag et al. (2021); One Rights was first proposed by Stucki and Sparks (2020) (noting that 'Increasing awareness of the interconnectedness of human, animal and

rights and (new) animal rights under a shared normative framework. On this understanding, animal rights are located not alongside or below human rights, but form an integral part of an updated and broadened conception of (post-)human rights. As will become clear throughout this book, the One Rights approach is based on the idea that, for all their nuances and differences, human rights and animal rights share a deep conceptual kinship and practical interdependence. The One Rights approach asserts that in a conceptual sense, human rights are animal rights and animal rights are human rights, and that in a practical sense, protecting human and animal rights in concert promises to yield better outcomes for humans, animals, and their shared planetary home.

1.4 Approach and Structure of the Book

This book brings together the seemingly disparate theories of human and animal rights, and consolidates them under a novel One Rights paradigm. It approaches the question whether animals can and should have human rights through an extensive interrogation of contemporary *human rights philosophy* and the justifications most commonly advanced therein. The animal question raises foundational issues about the nature and grounds of human rights. 'What are human rights, after all?'[73]—and why do all (and only) humans have them? These questions are surprisingly difficult to answer, not least because the concept of human rights is highly indeterminate and 'nearly criterionless'.[74] Human rights law—the legal field dealing with institutionalized human rights—is of little avail in finding answers to these fundamental questions. Perhaps because human rights are today so firmly entrenched in international and constitutional law, lawyers take the institution of human rights for granted and rarely feel the need to reflect on its foundations. As Samantha Besson notes, legal scholars tend to treat human rights as axiomatic or 'self-justificatory, an irreducible value that is not in need of further justification'.[75] Rather than looking to human rights law, the animal question leads us deep into human rights philosophy, which is tasked with justifying—giving reasons—for human rights.[76]

The philosophical landscape of human rights is marked by a bifurcation into *naturalistic* and *political conceptions*. Briefly put, naturalistic conceptions contemplate human rights as inherent moral rights deriving from some abstract human

---

ecosystem health has led to an integrative One Health (or One Welfare) approach in the natural sciences. Perhaps the time has come for a corresponding, holistic "One Rights" approach in law: human rights are animal rights, and animal rights are human rights').

[73] Hoffmann (2006), p. 406.

[74] Griffin (2008), p. 14.

[75] Besson (2018), p. 22.

[76] See Besson (2018), p. 23, 25; see also Sen (2004), p. 318 (noting that the 'difficult questions regarding ... human rights arise in the domain of ideas, before ... legalization occurs').

nature, whereas political conceptions centre on the practical functions of human rights as derived from concrete political practice. While naturalistic and political conceptions of human rights are often cast as opposing theoretical accounts, there is good reason to think that this dichotomy might be overdrawn.[77] Matthew Liao and Adam Etinson argue that naturalistic and political conceptions can be seen as mutually complementing rather than incompatible theories, since they address different aspects of human rights that do not necessarily overlap.[78] Indeed, naturalistic conceptions are primarily concerned with the nature and grounds of human rights (and with the innate qualities of their *individual* holders), whereas political conceptions are primarily concerned with the functional role of human rights (and the *institutional* dimension of their protection).

For the purposes of this book, it seems sensible to adopt a pluralistic approach that takes into account both naturalistic and political conceptions of human rights, in order to fathom both the conceptual and practical side of the animal question. Naturalistic theories, which analyse human rights in terms of their *conceptual nature*, are more pertinent for illuminating the conceptual issue whether animals can have human rights, whereas political theories, which explain human rights in terms of their *practical functions*, are more instructive for evaluating whether there are good practical reasons for affording animals human rights. Accordingly, this book pursues a two-pronged analysis that looks at animal rights through the lens of both naturalistic and political theories of human rights. In doing so, it takes a parsimonious approach that is agnostic to the issue of which conception of human rights is correct.[79] The aim of this book is not to determine the 'true' meaning of human rights, but rather, to examine whether animal rights can and should be an integral part of human rights, however properly understood.

Chapter 2 deals with the conceptual question whether animals *can* have human rights. It examines a range of naturalistic human rights theories in terms of their potential for providing a conceptual home for animal rights. It distinguishes between exceptionalist and non-exceptionalist conceptions of human rights: two families of naturalistic theories—resting on either 'old' or 'new humanism'—that differ in terms of their investment in human exceptionalism and their exclusiveness towards animals. As will be shown, the demarcation from and exclusion of animals is conceptually built-in to the first, exceptionalist conceptions, whereas the second, non-exceptionalist conceptions are only incidentally exclusive but conceptually open to animals. This chapter ultimately argues that the modern human rights paradigm is one of accidental yet inherent transspecies inclusivity, and therefore need not, indeed cannot consistently, be limited to the human species.

Chapter 3 addresses the practical question whether animals *should* have human rights through the lens of political conceptions and the functions they commonly attribute to human rights. This chapter argues that extending human rights to animals

---

[77] See generally Liao and Etinson (2012); Horn (2016).
[78] See Liao and Etinson (2012), p. 343.
[79] I thank Sergio Dellavalle for pointing this out.

is politically warranted for both principled (intrinsic) and prudential (instrumental) reasons. As a matter of justice, animals deserve and need human rights as a normative response to their experiences of violence, discrimination, and oppression. Moreover, animal rights also serve the indirect function of alleviating some of the gravest human rights threats such as dehumanization and environmental crises, and so have beneficial effects for humans too. This chapter thus challenges the dominant narrative of a principally antagonistic relationship between human and animal rights, and recasts it as one of synergism and interdependence. It argues that in light of their socio-political and ecological interconnectedness, human and animal rights are best protected in concert.

Chapter 4 synthesizes the insights drawn from naturalistic and political justifications of human and animal rights, and outlines the holistic One Rights approach as a new (post-)human rights paradigm for the Anthropocene.

Lastly, an important caveat is in order. The goal of this book is to introduce the novel concept of One Rights, and to substantiate its theoretical foundations along the dominant strands of human rights theory. In doing so, this book seeks to take the first steps towards a post-anthropocentric paradigm shift in the traditionally anthropocentric terrain of human rights. What this book does not aspire to do, however, is to develop a full-fledged and detailed account of One Rights as a legal paradigm. This would include, for example, an examination of what particular (human and nonhuman) right-holders hold which specific rights, what legal mechanisms may serve to resolve rights conflicts, and by what means to operationalize legal institutionalization, implementation, and enforcement. These questions are beyond the scope of this book, and may hopefully be the subject of future research.[80]

References

Abbey R (2017) Closer Kinships: Rortyan resources for animal rights. Contemp Polit Theory 16:1–18
Alston P (1979) Human rights and basic needs: a critical assessment. Revue des droits de l'homme 12:19–67
Alston P (1984) Conjuring up new human rights: a proposal for quality control. Am J Int Law 78:607–621
Besson S (2018) Justifications. In: Moeckli D, Shah S, Sivakumaran S (eds) International human rights law, 3rd edn. Oxford University Press, Oxford, pp 22–40
Bob C (ed) (2009) The international struggle for new human rights. University of Pennsylvania Press, Philadelphia
Boyd DR (2012) The environmental rights revolution: a global study of constitutions, human rights, and the environment. University of British Columbia Press, Vancouver
Brown C (1999) Universal human rights: a critique. In: Dunne T, Wheeler NJ (eds) Human rights in global politics. Cambridge University Press, Cambridge, pp 103–127
Brysk A, Stohl M (eds) (2017) Expanding human rights: 21st century norms and governance. Edward Elgar, Cheltenham

---

[80]I thank one of the anonymous reviewers for pointing this out.

References

Cavalieri P (2001) The animal question: why nonhuman animals deserve human rights. Oxford University Press, Oxford

Cavalieri P (2005) Are human rights human?. Logos 4.2 (spring 2005)

Chandler D (2016) The critique of human rights. In: Goodhart M (ed) Human rights: politics and practice, 3rd edn. Oxford University Press, Oxford, pp 110–126

Chapron G, Epstein Y, López-Bao JV (2019) A rights revolution for nature. Science 363:1392–1393

Cochrane A (2013) From human rights to sentient rights. Crit Rev Int Soc Polit Philosophy 16:655–675

Cruft R, Liao SM, Renzo M (2015) The philosophical foundations of human rights: an overview. In: Cruft R, Liao SM, Renzo M (eds) Philosophical foundations of human rights. Oxford University Press, Oxford, pp 1–41

Crutzen PJ (2002) Geology of mankind. Nature 415:23

Crutzen PJ, Stoermer EF (2000) The 'Anthropocene'. IGBP Newsl 41(May 2020):17–18

de Gouges O (1791) Déclaration des droits de la femme et de la citoyenne

Dembour MB (2017) Critiques. In: Moeckli D, Shah S, Sivakumaran S (eds) International human rights law, 3rd edn. Oxford University Press, Oxford, pp 41–62

Donaldson S, Kymlicka W (2011) Zoopolis: a political theory of animal rights. Oxford University Press, Oxford

Donnelly J (2013) Universal human rights in theory and practice, 3rd edn. Cornell University Press, Ithaca

Douzinas C (2000) The end of human rights: critical legal thought at the turn of the century. Hart, Oxford

Edmundson WA (2012) An introduction to rights, 2nd edn. Cambridge University Press, Cambridge

Fasel RN (2019) More equal than others: animals in the age of human rights aristocracy, PhD thesis. University of Cambridge

Fasel RN (2023) Direct democracy and animal rights. In: Peters A, Stilt K, Stucki S (eds) Oxford handbook of global animal law. Oxford University Press, Oxford (forthcoming)

Fellmeth AX (2016) Paradigms of international human rights law. Oxford University Press, Oxford

Francione GL, Charlton AE (2017) Animal rights. In: Kalof L (ed) Oxford handbook of animal studies. Oxford University Press, Oxford, pp 25–42

Gearty C (2009) Is human rights speciesist? In: Linzey A (ed) The link between animal abuse and human violence. Sussex Academic Press, Brighton, pp 175–183

Glendon MA (1991) Rights talk: the impoverishment of political discourse. Free Press, New York

Goodkin SL (1987) The evolution of animal rights. Columbia Human Rights Law Rev 18:259–288

Grear A (2007) Challenging corporate 'Humanity': legal disembodiment, embodiment and human rights. Human Rights Law Rev 7:511–543

Griffin J (2001) First steps in an account of human rights. Eur J Philosophy 9:306–327

Griffin J (2008) On human rights. Oxford University Press, Oxford

Hannum H (2016) Reinvigorating human rights for the twenty-first century. Human Rights Law Rev 16:409–451

Hannum H (2019) Rescuing human rights: a radically moderate approach. Cambridge University Press, Cambridge

Hoffmann FF (2006) 'Shooting into the Dark': toward a pragmatic theory of human rights (activism). Tex Int Law J 41:403–414

Hopgood S (2013) The endtimes of human rights. Cornell University Press, Ithaca, p 2013

Horn AS (2016) Moral and political conceptions of human rights: rethinking the distinction. Int J Human Rights 20:724–743

Hunt L (2007) Inventing human rights: a history. W.W. Norton & Company, New York

Ignatieff M (2001) Human rights as politics and idolatry. In: Gutmann A (ed) Human rights as politics and idolatry. Princeton University Press, Princeton, pp 3–98

Isiksel T (2016) The rights of man and the rights of the man-made: corporations and human rights. Human Rights Q 38:294–349
Jowitt J (2016) Monkey see, Monkey Sue? Gewirth's principle of generic consistency and rights for non-human agents. Trinity Coll Law Rev 19:71–96
Kotzé LJ (2019) Editorial: coloniality, neoliberalism and the anthropocene. J Human Rights Environ 10:1–6
Kymlicka W (2018) Human rights without human supremacism. Canadian J Philosophy 48:763–792
Kymlicka W, Donaldson S (2018) Rights. In: Gruen L (ed) Critical terms for animal studies. University of Chicago Press, Chicago, pp 320–336
Lafont C (2016) Should we take the 'Human' out of human rights? Human dignity in a corporate world. Ethics Int Aff 30:233–252
Liao SM, Etinson A (2012) Political and naturalistic conceptions of human rights: a false polemic? J Moral Philosophy 9:327–352
MacKinnon CA (2006) Are women human? And other international dialogues. Harvard University Press, Cambridge
O'Connell P (2018) On the human rights question. Human Rights Q 40:962–988
Peters A (2016) Liberté, Égalité, Animalité: human-animal comparisons in law. Transnatl Environ Law 5:25–53
Peters A (2018) Rights of human and Nonhuman animals: complementing the universal declaration of human rights. AJIL Unbound 112:355–360
Pietrzykowski T (2020) Animal rights. In: von Arnauld A, von der Decken K, Susi M (eds) Cambridge handbook of new human rights: recognition, novelty, rhetoric. Cambridge University Press, Cambridge, pp 243–252
Pocar V (1992) Animal rights: a socio-legal perspective. J Law Soc 19:214–230
Purdy J (2015) After nature: a politics for the anthropocene. Harvard University Press, Cambridge
Rockström J et al (2009) A safe operating space for humanity. Nature 461:472–475
Salt HS (1892) Animals' rights considered in relation to social progress. George Bell & Sons, London
Schulz WF, Raman S (2020) The coming good society: why new realities demand new rights. Harvard University Press, Cambridge
Sebo J (2022) Saving animals, saving ourselves: why animals matter for pandemics, climate change, and other catastrophes. Oxford University Press, Oxford
Sen A (2004) Elements of a theory of human rights. Philosophy Public Aff 32:315–356
Sparks T, Kurki V, Stucki S (2020) Editorial: animal rights – interconnections with human rights and the environment. J Human Rights Environ 11:149–155
Stone CD (1972) Should trees have standing? – Toward legal rights for natural objects. South Calif Law Rev 45:450–501
Stucki S (2020) Towards a theory of legal animal rights: simple and fundamental rights. Oxford J Legal Stud 40:533–560
Stucki S (2023) Animal warfare law and the need for an animal law of peace: a comparative reconstruction. Am J Comp Law 71 (forthcoming)
Stucki S, Kurki V (2020) Animal rights. In: Sellers M, Kirste S (eds) Encyclopedia of the philosophy of law and social philosophy. Springer, Dordrecht. https://doi.org/10.1007/978-94-007-6730-0_407-1
Stucki S, Sparks T (2020) The Elephant in the (Court)Room: interdependence of human and animal rights in the anthropocene. EJIL:Talk, 9 June 2020. https://www.ejiltalk.org/the-elephant-in-the-courtroom-interdependence-of-human-and-animal-rights-in-the-anthropocene/
Sumner LW (1987) The moral foundation of rights. Oxford University Press, Oxford
Susi M (2020) Novelty in new human rights: the decrease in universality and abstractness thesis. In: von Arnauld A, von der Decken K, Susi M (eds) Cambridge handbook of new human rights: recognition, novelty, rhetoric. Cambridge University Press, Cambridge, pp 21–33

References

Tasioulas J (2019) Saving human rights from human rights law. Vanderbilt J Transnatl Law 52:1167–1207

Taylor T (1792) A vindication of the rights of brutes. Pall-Mall, London

Vincent A (2010) The politics of human rights. Oxford University Press, Oxford

von Arnauld A, von der Decken K, Susi M (eds) (2020) Cambridge handbook of new human rights: recognition, novelty, rhetoric. Cambridge University Press, Cambridge

von der Decken K, Koch N (2020) Recognition of new human rights: phases, techniques and the approach of 'differentiated traditionalism'. In: von Arnauld A, von der Decken K, Susi M (eds) Cambridge handbook of new human rights: recognition, novelty, rhetoric. Cambridge University Press, Cambridge, pp 7–20

Wellman C (1999) The proliferation of rights: moral progress or empty rhetoric? Westview Press, Boulder

Wills J (2020) Animal rights, legal personhood and cognitive capacity: addressing 'Levelling-Down' concerns. J Human Rights Environ 11:199–223

Winston M (2007) Human rights as Moral Rebellion and social construction. J Human Rights 6:279–305

Wollstonecraft M (1792) A vindication of the rights of woman: with strictures on moral and political subjects. Thomas and Andrews, Boston

Wuerth I (2017) International law in the post-human rights era. Tex Law Rev 96:279–349

Zinsstag J, Schelling E, Crump L, Whittaker M, Tanner M, Stephen C (eds) (2021) One health: the theory and practice of integrated health approaches, 2nd edn. CABI, Wallingford

Open Access This chapter is licensed under the terms of the Creative Commons Attribution 4.0 International License (http://creativecommons.org/licenses/by/4.0/), which permits use, sharing, adaptation, distribution and reproduction in any medium or format, as long as you give appropriate credit to the original author(s) and the source, provide a link to the Creative Commons license and indicate if changes were made.

The images or other third party material in this chapter are included in the chapter's Creative Commons license, unless indicated otherwise in a credit line to the material. If material is not included in the chapter's Creative Commons license and your intended use is not permitted by statutory regulation or exceeds the permitted use, you will need to obtain permission directly from the copyright holder.

Chapter 2
Naturalistic Conceptions of Human and Animal Rights: From Human Exceptionalism to Transspecies Universalism

> Human rights in the real world are proving far less attached to their Enlightenment baggage than are the intellectuals who guard its theory. *MacKinnon (2000), p. 711.*

This chapter investigates whether the extension of human rights to animals can be placed on a sound conceptual footing. Can (nonhuman) animals have human rights? The starting point of this inquiry is the 'traditional'[1] or 'orthodox'[2] understanding of human rights, which is the naturalistic conception.[3] This much can be said already: considering the contested nature and philosophical foundations of human rights, there cannot be a simple, let alone single, answer to the animal question.

2.1 Setting the Stage for the 'Theater of Human Law'[4]

Human rights are most commonly understood as inherent and universal fundamental rights that every human being has simply in virtue of being human.[5] This is called the naturalistic conception, because—like the idea of natural rights—it derives human rights from *human nature* and justifies them with reference to some essential

---

[1] Raz (2010), p. 323.
[2] Beitz (2004), p. 196; van Duffel (2013), p. 32.
[3] On the naturalistic conception of human rights, see generally Beitz (2009), p. 48ff.
[4] Tercer Juzgado de Garantías de Mendoza 3 November 2016, Expte Nro P-72.254/15 (noting that animals are currently 'involuntary actors in the theater of human law', and that extending to them fundamental rights is 'the best act of inclusion' we can do).
[5] See, paradigmatically, Gewirth (1982b), p. 41 ('We may assume, as true by definition, that human rights are rights that all persons have simply insofar as they are human'); Griffin (2001), p. 2 ('A human right is one that a person has, not in virtue of any special status or relation to others, but simply in virtue of being human'); for an analysis of the commonplace formula 'simply in virtue of being human', see Fasel (2018); Gardner (2008).

feature of humanity.[6] Virtually all naturalistic conceptions operate under the (oftentimes implicit and seemingly self-evident) assumption that 'being human' is both a necessary and sufficient condition for having human rights.[7] That is, human rights are naturally thought of as rights that belong to *all* and *only* humans *because* they are human.[8]

From the outset, human rights is a firmly *humanist* (human-centred, i.e., anthropocentric)[9] project whose foundational-justificational nexus to humanity appears both radically *inclusive* as regards all humans (qua being human) and, simultaneously, *exclusive* as regards all other animals (qua being nonhuman).[10] Notwithstanding this *prima facie* 'exclusive nature' of human rights,[11] the question remains whether a necessary conceptual rather than a merely conventional[12] or even arbitrary link exists between human rights and humanity. As we will see, the degree and (inherent or incidental) nature of exclusivity infused into human rights largely depends on the underlying conception of human nature that informs any given naturalistic theory.

---

[6] See Pollmann (2014), p. 121; Raz (2010), p. 323 (noting that naturalistic theories generally rely 'on no contingent fact except laws of nature, the nature of humanity and that the right-holder is a human being'); the naturalistic conception is often described as a 'modernized, secularized form of natural rights' (Cruft et al. (2015), p. 2). See e.g. Tasioulas (2012a), p. 26 (noting 'strong continuities between human rights and the traditional idea of natural rights'); Nickel (2007), p. 12 (human rights as 'the recycling and updating of old ideas within a new, transnational context').

[7] See Pollmann (2014), p. 126 (noting the self-evident and central presupposition that 'one has to belong to the human species to be a bearer of human rights').

[8] See e.g. Edmundson (2012), p. 154 ('Human rights, one would think, are rights possessed by all (and only) humans, who possess these rights simply in virtue of their humanity'); van Duffel (2013), p. 49 (noting that 'Intuitions regarding human rights ... are that *all* and *only* human beings have human rights'); Beauchamp (2011), p. 205 ('The natural reading of "human rights" is rights for humans only'); a notable exception is Feinberg (1973), p. 85, who defines human rights as 'generically moral rights of a fundamentally important kind held equally by all human beings, unconditionally and unalterably' while emphasizing that this definition 'includes the phrase "*all* human beings" but does not say "*only* human beings," so that a human right held by animals is not excluded by definition'.

[9] If humanism is the 'philosophy of which man is the center and sanction' (Lamont (1997), p. 12), it is anthropocentric by definition; on the 'philosophical speciesism' and anthropocentrism permeating the discourse of human rights, see generally Gearty (2009, 2010); Naffine (2012), p. 68; Grear (2011), p. 24ff.

[10] See Cavalieri (2001), p. 70; Corbey (2013), pp. 67–69 (noting that humanist 'discourse on human rights ... proclaimed a new, more inclusive demarcation of morally respectable beings by a continuing exclusion of others').

[11] Cochrane (2013), p. 655.

[12] cf. Stone (1972), p. 453 (noting that 'We are inclined to suppose the rightlessness of rightless "things" to be a decree of Nature, not a legal convention acting in support of some status quo').

2.2 Who Is the 'Human' of Human Rights?

To further explore the nexus between human rights and human nature, we need to inquire into the operative understanding of 'being human' (simply in virtue of which human rights are had).[13] As James Griffin has noted, 'there is little agreement about the relevant sense of "human"',[14] and accordingly, naturalistic accounts tend to gesture towards different manifestations of 'the human'. Two distinctions are to be made in particular: first, between biological and essentialist understandings of 'being human' and second, between exceptionalist and non-exceptionalist conceptions of humanness.

2.2.1 The 'Biological Human' and the 'Essential Human'

William Edmundson points out that the phrase 'human rights' is ambiguous and can be understood to mean 'those rights belonging to human beings as such' or 'those rights paradigmatically attributed to human beings in virtue of their possessing important characteristics and capacities'.[15] This ambiguity translates to a distinction between a *direct, purely biological* and an *indirect, essentialist or placeholder* sense of 'being human'.

In the first sense, 'being human' simply refers to the biological fact of being born a human. Biological humanness is typically relied upon for practical—and especially legal—purposes, as it offers a clear-cut criterion for operationalizing the normative imperative that 'all members of the species *Homo sapiens*' must be human rights-holders.[16] This finds paradigmatic expression in the preamble of the Universal Declaration of Human Rights, which recognizes the equal and inalienable rights of 'all members of the human family'. While the biological human may conveniently serve as the embodied locus of human rights, it does not provide an adequate basis for the philosophical purposes of *justifying* human rights. Justificatory theories are tasked with clarifying the complex relationship between human rights and human nature. As Jack Donnelly puts it, 'How does being human give one rights?'[17] The biologistic determination merely asserts that all humans *have* human rights, but does not proffer (or even purport to offer) a philosophical justification of human rights and

---

[13] Paradigmatically Tasioulas (2012b), p. 37 ('human rights are rights possessed by all human beings (*however properly characterized*)' (emphasis added)).

[14] Griffin (2001), p. 2.

[15] Edmundson (2012), p. 154.

[16] Donnelly (2013), p. 10; Nino (1991), p. 35 (noting that for 'practical purposes we need a concept of *human* being defined in biological terms' that provides a hard, 'all-or-nothing' criterion for determining human rights-holders).

[17] Donnelly (2013), p. 13.

reasons as to *why* (all and only) humans have them.[18] Moreover, it is today widely accepted that purely biological facts—such as 'race', sex, or species membership—are normatively irrelevant and cannot per se justify differential treatment.[19] To avoid the well-established charge of (unqualified) speciesism,[20] justificatory theories will thus typically attempt to adhere to some form of *species neutrality requirement*, according to which an 'adequate account of right-holding should provide a criterion that does not in principle exclude any being simply on the basis of their species'.[21]

Rather than relying on a purely biological sense of being human, most naturalistic accounts refer to something else: the essential human.[22] For essentialist naturalistic theories, 'being human' serves as a convenient, albeit not quite accurate and somewhat misleading shorthand for some other essential quality that is possessed by all (and/or only) humans *and* is normatively relevant for grounding human rights.[23] Human rights, so justified, are thus actually 'human qua X' rights, with X signifying some essential human (and human rights-relevant) property.[24] However, if 'being human' is merely a placeholder for a rights-grounding essential human feature, this begs the question: which aspect of human nature is it that grounds human rights?

---

[18] See Bilchitz (2009), p. 52f (noting that this kind of biologistic 'reasoning is wholly unpersuasive', as it 'involves simple assertion without justifying why the category of homo sapiens is sufficient to determine worth and the type of treatment human beings are to be accorded').

[19] See e.g. Nino (1991), p. 35 (noting that 'it is difficult to see how a purely biological fact . . . could be morally relevant. That would be similar to the racist standpoint'); Liao (2012), p. 276 (noting that 'membership in the class of human beings is more like membership in a racial group in being a purely biological relation'); Bilchitz (2009), p. 53 (arguing that speciesism is an unjustifiable prejudice akin to racism and sexism).

[20] 'Speciesism . . . is a prejudice or attitude of bias in favor of the interests of members of one's own species and against those of members of other species.' Singer (1995), p. 6.

[21] Cruft et al. (2015), p. 9; Liao (2010), p. 162 (noting that justifications of human rights should 'meet the Species Neutrality Requirement so as to not be speciesist').

[22] Naturalistic accounts of human rights are typically essentialist, in that they operate under an essentialist mode of reasoning which assumes that 'the human' has a true and essential nature, a metaphysical essence, that determines what it essentially means to be human. See Naffine (2012), p. 69f.

[23] Paradigmatically Griffin (2008), p. 34f ('"Human" cannot . . . mean simply being a member of the species *Homo sapiens*. . . . by the word "human" in the phrase "human rights" we should mean, roughly, a functioning human agent'); see also Miller (2015), p. 234 (noting that 'it is somewhat misleading to say that being human is the *ground* of human rights . . . The ground of human rights is rather the feature, universally possessed by human beings, that justifies these rights').

[24] The universalist formula that 'all humans have human rights' is thus the conclusion of an enthymeme (the unstated major premise is that human rights are grounded in X; the unstated minor premise is that all humans have X; the stated conclusion is that all humans have human rights); according to Pollmann (2014), p. 127, this kind of reasoning is bound to be circular, because the conclusion is already presupposed in the premises. That is, X in premise 1 is determined in a manner that is predetermined by premise 2, in order to reach the desired conclusion—the conclusion thus shaping the major premise from the outset.

2.2.2 The 'Exceptional Human' and the 'Typical Human'

In identifying a rights-grounding essential human feature, naturalistic theories may either reference what might be called the 'exceptional human' or the 'typical human'. That is, they may rely on a particular aspect of either *unique* or *ordinary* human nature. Generally speaking, and drawing on dehumanization psychology,[25] there are two distinct conceptions of human nature that differ in terms of their investment in the idea of human exceptionalism.[26] We may call them the *exceptionalist* and *non-exceptionalist* conceptions of human nature. The exceptionalist conception describes a *special* human nature; it defines *uniquely* human properties that are believed to separate humans from animals. Nick Haslam calls this the 'comparative sense of humanness', as it determines human nature relative to (a definitionally distinct) animal nature.[27] The second, non-exceptionalist conception captures human nature *simpliciter*; it defines *typically* human characteristics that are central to humans, regardless of whether these features are shared with other animals or not. This non-comparative sense of humanness is thus irrelative to animal nature and also indifferent to human exceptionality.

Accordingly, depending on the underlying conception of human nature, there is an important distinction to be made among essentialist naturalistic theories (in which 'human' serves as a placeholder for some essential truth about human nature): between exceptionalist conceptions of human rights (identifying some essential *metaphysical* or rationalist truth about *extraordinary* human nature) and non-exceptionalist conceptions (identifying some essential *materialist* or anthropological truth about *ordinary* human nature).[28] Exceptionalist conceptions ground human rights in unique human nature and justify human rights with reference to some special human property, typically relating to the rational nature of humans. By contrast, non-exceptionalist conceptions ground human rights in typical human nature and justify human rights with reference to some empirical (and more profane) aspect of the *conditio humana*, such as basic needs, interests, capabilities, or vulnerability.

In the following sections, I will more closely examine these two families of naturalistic theories with regard to their exclusive or potentially inclusive implications for animals. As may already be intuited, the exclusivity or inclusivity of human rights varies greatly between these two strands of naturalistic theories, and is ultimately predetermined by the underlying conception of (unique or typical) human nature.

---

[25] The psychological study of dehumanization is relevant in this context, because all phenomena of dehumanization minimally involve the 'denial of humanness', and therefore require a clear understanding of 'what constitutes humanness'. See Haslam (2014), p. 35f.
[26] On these two distinct senses of humanness, see generally Haslam (2006).
[27] Haslam (2006), p. 256.
[28] See also Pollmann (2014), p. 123f (distinguishing among naturalistic theories between metaphysical/theological, rationalist/transcendental, and materialistic/anthropological accounts).

2.3 Exceptionalist Conceptions of Human Rights and the Decline of Old Humanism

2.3.1 Overview

The first, more senior family of essentialist naturalistic theories grounds human rights in a *rationalist* notion of *unique* human nature. Exceptionalist conceptions are based on a rationalist-humanist view that emphasizes human specialness, and subscribe to an abstract image of 'the human' as *animal rationale* whose capacity for reason sets her (or rather, him[29]) apart from animals.[30] Paradigmatically, Margaret MacDonald states that 'Reason is the great leveller or elevator' and that it is by having the natural quality of being rational that 'men resemble each other and differ from the brutes.'[31] The justifications advanced for human rights revolve around a cluster of interrelated, rationality- and autonomy-based concepts, such as personhood,[32] the capacity for moral agency (i.e., the 'capacity to act in light of moral reasons'),[33] or human dignity. What these justificatory approaches have in common is that they typically single out some variant of the rational nature of humans as the essential feature which grounds human rights of all (and only) human beings.[34]

For example, Alan Gewirth bases human rights on 'the necessary conditions of human action', and holds that they pertain equally to 'all humans who have the

---

[29] As critical scholars point out, 'the "man" of human rights is literally a Western white middle-class man who ... has stamped his image on law and human rights and has become the measure of all things and people.' Douzinas (2000), p. 165.

[30] See Naffine (2012), p. 83; Murphy (2011), p. 575 (noting that 'strains of religious, secular, existential, and Marxist humanism have tended to circumscribe the category of the human with reference to the themes of reason, autonomy, judgment, and freedom'); Schulz & Raman (2020), p. 149 (noting that traditional naturalistic theories hold that 'not only are humans higher in importance than animals but that animals lack the qualities, such as reason or inherent dignity, that would make them eligible for rights in the first place').

[31] MacDonald (1984), p. 25; similarly, Maritain (2011), p. 66, 100 (stating that the human person 'is an animal gifted with reason' and that 'Man is an animal ... but unlike other animals ... He exists not merely physically; there is in him a richer and nobler existence; he has spiritual superexistence through knowledge').

[32] The legal and philosophical concept of personhood is ambiguous and elusive. Grounding human rights in personhood may thus further complicate, rather than resolve, the matter of finding a coherent justificatory basis for human rights. See Ohlin (2005), pp. 248f (arguing that 'Personhood is a placeholder for deeper concepts that ground our moral intuitions about human rights. Consequently, human rights arguments are obscured by their reliance on the concept of the person.' He further notes that 'if the concept of the person is deployed as a mere placeholder for a conclusion, it cannot simultaneously serve as a *reason* for granting rights, on pain of circularity.' Ibid., p. 218).

[33] Liao (2010), p. 164.

[34] See Cochrane (2013), p. 660 (noting that it is commonly held that human rights 'identify and protect something special and unique about humanity'); Tasioulas (2012a), p. 13 (noting that 'Our capacity to choose and pursue a conception of the good life is the relevant dimension along which the human rights tradition regards humanity as set apart from non-human animals').

minimal degree of *rationality needed for action*.'[35] James Griffin notes that 'Human life is different from the life of other animals' in that humans are agents with a conception of, and the mental abilities to pursue, a good life.[36] On his account, human rights are protections of 'our *normative agency*' or of an 'essential feature of *personhood*',[37] and grounded in two basic human interests: *autonomy* and *liberty*.[38] Carl Wellman also starts from the observation that 'Normal adult human beings differ from all the other beings known to us in a way that commands our respect', and that there 'is something about human nature ... that confers upon human beings a very special moral status.' On this basis, he identifies '*practical reason*' and 'the *capacity for moral action* of any normal adult human being' as a necessary condition for the possession of human rights.[39]

2.3.2 Programmatic Exclusivity

Exceptionalist conceptions of human rights are reflective and expressive of traditional, *anthropocentric* humanism[40]—what has been variously called 'human supremacism',[41] 'human chauvinism',[42] 'species-narcissism',[43] 'human racism'[44] or, more generally, 'speciesism' and 'anthropocentrism'.[45] Old humanism is underpinned by a 'belief in human exceptionality'[46] and thus foundationally invested in the idea of *human exceptionalism*—the 'ideological belief system of human supremacy' that considers humans fundamentally distinct from and superior

---

[35] Gewirth (1982a), p. 5, 8 (emphasis added).
[36] Griffin (2008), p. 32f.
[37] Griffin (2010), p. 345f (emphasis added).
[38] Griffin (2012), p. 10 ('The two basic human interests grounding human rights ... are the two constituents of normative agency: autonomy and liberty').
[39] Wellman (2011), p. 21f (emphasis added).
[40] According to Weitzenfeld and Joy (2014), p. 5, the dominant tradition of humanism since the Enlightenment can be characterized as anthropocentric humanism 'due to its ideological commitment to conceptualizing human being over and against animal being'.
[41] Kymlicka (2018); Patterson (2002), p. 3ff ('human supremacy').
[42] Routley and Routley (1979); Cavalieri (2001), p. 70.
[43] Benton (1988), p. 7.
[44] Eckersley (1998), p. 169 (understood as 'systematic prejudice against nonhuman species').
[45] Weitzenfeld and Joy (2014), p. 4 (defining anthropocentrism as 'a belief system, an ideology of human supremacy that advocates privileging humans' and 'functions to maintain the centrality and priority of human existence').
[46] Pietrzykowski (2017), p. 49.

to animals.[47] Exceptionalist accounts inherit old humanism's commitment to human exceptionalism, and—whether explicitly or implicitly—inscribe the exclusion of animals into the conceptual fabric of human rights. This is because they rest on an image of (unique) human nature that is precisely constructed in contradistinction to animals as the antithetical other, where animals serve only as 'markers and evidence of human distinctiveness and elevation.'[48] Given this built-in demarcation from animals, exceptionalist conceptions of human rights demarcate a nearly impenetrable zone of exclusivity around humans.[49]

Even so, there exists a certain grey area at the margins of human rights so conceived. Many exceptionalist accounts (especially of the strictly rationalist variant) are facially non-speciesist, in that they advance capacity- rather than species-based justifications of human rights.[50] For example, Matthew Liao considers it a virtue of his account 'that it allows virtually all human beings to be rightholders *without being speciesist*'. This is because it 'allows non-human entities such as aliens, possibly Great Apes ... to be rightholders, if these entities have the physical (usually genetic) basis for moral agency.'[51] Similarly, James Griffin makes room for the (hypothetical) possibility of other-than-human creatures having the high intelligence necessary for moral agency: 'If so, we should have to consider how *human* rights would have to be adapted to fit them.'[52] Suchlike theoretical concessions to species-neutrality gesture towards a certain (albeit low) degree of permeability that could possibly allow for some highly intelligent animals (such as great apes or whales)[53] to break through the programmatic exclusivity of human rights. In reality, however, these rationality-based justifications of human rights set such a high and

---

[47] Costello and Hodson (2014), p. 177f; Gruen (2011), p. 4ff (human uniqueness and human superiority as distinctive claims of human exceptionalism); Weitzenfeld and Joy (2014), p. 5f (identifying human exceptionalism as a key premise of anthropocentric humanism).

[48] Rossello (2016), p. 752 (calling this 'inclusive exclusion', whereby animals are simultaneously *included* in the construal of a special human identity and *excluded* from the higher normative status so construed); MacKinnon (2005), p. 266 (calling this 'definition-by-distinction'); Weitzenfeld and Joy (2014), p. 7 (noting that anthropocentric humanism is engaged in a 'boundary project of delimiting "the human" from "the animal" ... in which what is essential to and valuable about humanity is defined by what all animal others lack'); see generally Horkheimer and Adorno (2002), p. 203f ('Throughout European history the idea of the human being has been expressed in contradistinction to the animal. The latter's lack of reason is the proof of human dignity. So insistently and unanimously has this antithesis been recited ... that few other ideas are so fundamental to Western anthropology').

[49] On the exclusivity of old humanist—or Aristocratic—human rights accounts, see also Fasel (2019b), p. 94f.

[50] For example, for an application of Gewirth's agency account to animal agents, see Jowitt (2020).

[51] Liao (2012), p. 265, 272.

[52] Griffin (2008), p. 32.

[53] See e.g. D'Amato and Chopra (1991), p. 21, 27 (making a 'minimal case' for extending the single most fundamental human right—the right to life—to whales, notably because whales are a species 'that scientists speculate has higher than human intelligence').

anthropocentric bar that, de facto, *only* (but likely not *all*) humans as real-world entities will qualify as right-holders.[54]

2.3.3 Problems of Exceptionalist Accounts

Exclusive accounts of human rights that rely on human exceptionalism in the form of agency, rationality, or dignity are vulnerable to a range of well-known problems and objections.

2.3.3.1 Strictly Rationalist Accounts and the Problem of Marginal Cases

First of all, rationalist justifications of human rights face the obvious problem that not all humans are rational agents (so-called 'marginal cases'). Lack of rationality and agency is an inevitable part of the human condition, with infants not possessing such capacities yet, people with severe dementia not anymore, and some mentally severely impaired humans never possessing them at all. Human rights exceptionalism thus collides with empirical reality, which is populated by people who do not conform to the 'exaggerated caricature' of the human as 'rational, self-directing, wholly autonomous individual possessing moral agency'.[55]

The problem here is that the 'human' in human rights serves as a placeholder for an essential feature that likely *only*, but certainly *not all* human beings actually possess. Rationalist accounts thus run the risk of being *under-inclusive*, since strictly speaking, many humans (along with animals) would not qualify to have human rights.[56] As Henry McCloskey has so bluntly put it, 'even if the theory of natural law could be established ... infants, lunatics and idiots are not subject to it as rational agents any more than is an intelligent dog or ape.'[57] Indeed, some rationalist theorists bring this 'undesirable consequence'[58] to its logical conclusion, by

---

[54] cf. Frey (1988), p. 199 (noting that using 'human-centred criteria' for determining normative status might be considered 'indirect speciesist'); Fjellstrom (2002), p. 70 (noting that reliance on 'human-centred validational tools' is speciesist to the extent that 'they are construed to yield arguments that assure ethical precedence for humans').

[55] Quinn and Arstein-Kerslake (2012), p. 37; see also Douzinas (2000), p. 237 (noting that the 'legal subject is the caricature of the real person, a cartoon-like figure which, as all caricature, exaggerates certain features and characteristics and totally misses others'); Fineman (2008), p. 19 (noting that rationalist law is 'built upon myths of autonomy and independence and thus fails to reflect the vulnerable as well as dependent nature of the human condition').

[56] See Tasioulas (2012a), p. 14 (noting that rationalist accounts suffer from an acute problem: 'the potential exclusion from the protection of human rights of all human beings who are not agents'); on the problem of underinclusiveness, see Fasel (2018), p. 474f.

[57] McCloskey (1965), p. 124.

[58] Nino (1991), p. 36 (noting that a rationalist grounding of human rights has the 'undesirable consequence' that, because 'the properties in question are not of an "all-or-nothing" but of a gradual

asserting that *not all humans* are human right-holders.[59] For example, James Griffin concludes that it seems best 'to reserve the term "human rights" for normative agents' and that 'human rights should not be extended to infants, to patients in an irreversible coma or with advanced dementia, or to the severely mentally defective'.[60] Likewise, Carl Wellman submits that 'one can and should accept the conclusion that only human beings defined not as members of a biological species but in the morally relevant sense as persons with the normal human capacities for moral action could possess any moral human right.'[61]

While the exclusion of human and animal non-agents alike may be philosophically consistent under a strictly rationalist conception, human rights are then really not *human* (qua human) rights, but rather, (partly human qua) agent or person rights.[62] This 'elitist outlook'[63] is hardly the best explanation of the modern human rights paradigm. Not only is it widely considered morally reprehensible, as it undercuts the protective reach of human rights to some of society's most vulnerable, non-paradigmatic members such as children, the elderly, or mentally disabled people.[64] Strictly rationalist accounts are also at odds with our ordinary and codified understanding of *universal* human rights as rights that every human being has irrespective of her individual particularities, including physical or mental (dis)-abilities.[65] The disconnect between rationalist justifications of human rights and contemporary human rights law is particularly apparent with regard to the UN Convention on the Rights of Persons with Disabilities[66] or the UN Convention on

---

kind ... *human* beings would be entitled to rights of different degrees according to their rationality').

[59] See van Duffel (2013), p. 48 (noting that faced with the 'obvious objection that not all human beings are agents ... some theorists have simply bitten the bullet and maintained that not all human beings, only agents, have rights').

[60] Griffin (2008), p. 94f (further stating that 'We should see children as acquiring rights in stages—the stages in which they acquire agency').

[61] Wellman (2011), p. 22.

[62] See Cruft et al. (2015), p. 12 (noting that 'Instead of justifying the existence of rights that all human beings possess qua human being, they justify something different: rights that all persons possess qua persons'); Buchanan (2011), p. 213f ('If "humanity" refers to personhood ... then we might decide that what we have called human rights would be more accurately called *persons' rights*.').

[63] Nino (1991), p. 36.

[64] See Cochrane (2013), p. 660f; Donaldson and Kymlicka (2011), p. 23.

[65] See Masferrer and García-Sánchez (2016), p. 5 (noting that 'The legal system aims to ensure respect for the basic rights of individuals, not because they are intelligent or particularly skilled or talented, but just because of their human condition'); Dupré (2015), p. 22 (noting that human rights law aims to include 'all human beings within its protective scope, regardless of the degree of self-awareness of their humanity or their ability to take rational decisions affecting their life or death').

[66] See e.g. Quinn and Arstein-Kerslake (2012), p. 38ff.

2.3 Exceptionalist Conceptions of Human Rights and the Decline of Old Humanism

the Rights of the Child (which stresses not children's potentiality for agency but their vulnerability[67]).[68]

2.3.3.2 Generically Rationalist Accounts and the Problem of (Qualified) Speciesism

If lack of rationality is not accepted as a reason for pre-, post-, or never-rational humans *not* to have human rights, how can human rights be denied to animals on those very grounds? At this juncture, rationalist accounts run into the problem of (in)consistency, as has been abundantly pointed out by the argument from marginal cases or species overlap.[69] The logic of the argument goes as follows: to the extent that the cognitive abilities of some human and nonhuman animals are the same or similar, the principle of equal treatment[70] requires either excluding, together with animals, such humans that do not meet the rationality criterion, or (if the latter are included) to equally waive the rationality-prerequisite for animals with comparable cognitive constitutions.[71]

Faced with this 'unpalatable dilemma',[72] defenders of exceptionalist human rights (of *all and only* humans) frequently put forward that, whether actually present in an individual or not, the capacity for agency or rationality constitutes a *generic* feature of humans. According to this line of argument, what matters is that human beings *normally* or *potentially* possess the capacity for rationality, and belonging to the *kind* of beings that typically have the human rights-relevant properties is sufficient for having human rights.[73] I will not reiterate the many meticulous

---

[67] As pointed out by Griffin (2008), p. 85.

[68] See also Kymlicka (2018), p. 778; even with regard to the Universal Declaration of Human Rights—despite its rationalistic overtone—the 'majority of the drafters had come to see the phrase "endowed with reason and conscience" as problematic ... The drafters had good reasons for not wanting to make the possession of reason and conscience a prerequisite for having inalienable rights'. Morsink (1999), p. 299.

[69] On the argument from marginal cases, see e.g. Gruen (2011), p. 64ff; Bilchitz (2009), p. 56ff; Tanner (2009); Dombrowski (1997); on the argument from species overlap, see Horta (2014); Wills (2020).

[70] See e.g. Rachels (1990), p. 182 (the principle of equality 'implies that the interests of non-humans should receive the *same* consideration as the comparable interests of humans').

[71] See e.g. Singer (2009), p. 574 (noting that 'attempts to draw a moral line on the basis of cognitive ability ... will require either that we exclude some humans – for example, those who are profoundly mentally retarded – or that we include some nonhuman animals – those whose levels of cognitive ability are equal or superior to the lowest level found in human beings'); Kymlicka (2018), p. 779 (highlighting that this 'is a structural problem for supremacist theories. Given the continuities between humans and animals in their interests, capacities and subjectivities, there simply is no way to justify throwing animals under the bus without simultaneously throwing some humans under the bus (or at least dramatically increasing the risks that they will be thrown under the bus)').

[72] Nino (1991), p. 36.

[73] See Liao (2010), p. 161f (with further references).

objections formulated against this sort of argument from kinds,[74] potentiality,[75] or species normality.[76] Suffice it to say that the conflation of membership in the human species and possession of a 'status-conferring intrinsic property'[77] reintroduces, through the backdoor, biological humanness as a morally relevant fact and is thus vulnerable to the charge of *(qualified) speciesism.*[78] By infusing rational agency into the generic nature of human beings, *all* humans are fictionally attributed—and treated as if they possessed—the human rights-grounding quality, simply in virtue of belonging to a species that typically has it.[79] This shift from a capacity- to a group-based foundation of human rights runs counter to the notion of *moral individualism,* which rejects the idea of treating humans—or animals—not as individuals but rather as specimens of their kind or group.[80] Indeed, most human rights scholars would agree that 'it is precisely the fact that people are being judged on the basis of their kind rather than their individual merits that make racism and sexism so objectionable.'[81]

The bottom line of these critiques is that there does not seem to be an empirically verifiable feature or capacity that *all and only* humans actually possess *and* that is relevant for grounding human rights.[82] In the end, biological humanness re-emerges and remains as the only hard, all-or-nothing natural attribute that works to include all humans while simultaneously excluding all animals. Exclusive human rights can thus ultimately be operationalized only by resorting to speciesism, that is, by claiming that membership in the human species is either directly morally significant

---

[74] See e.g. Nobis (2004); McMahan (2005), p. 358 (rightly noting that the kind-argument is generally only embraced when deployed to *level up* humans, but not consistently applied if it would require *levelling down* human individuals).

[75] See e.g. Feinberg and Baum Levenbook (1993), p. 205ff (succinctly noting, by way of a *reductio ad absurdum*, that 'everything is potentially everything else', and that it is a logical error to 'deduce *actual* rights from merely *potential* (but not yet actual) qualification for those rights'); Rothhaar (2014); Tooley (2009), p. 35ff; Perrett (2000).

[76] See generally McMahan (2002).

[77] The specific property which is relevant for having moral status in general and human rights in particular. See McMahan (2005), p. 355.

[78] Qualified speciesism means that species membership is counterfactually correlated with morally significant characteristics. See Rachels (1990), p. 184ff; LaFollette and Shanks (1996), p. 42f.

[79] See McMahan (2005), p. 355f; McCloskey (1965), p. 123 (noting that 'The general tendency has been to maintain that free agents and potential free agents have rights, with idiots, and all born from human parents being treated as potentially free agents, although many are obviously not such').

[80] On moral individualism, see Rachels (1990), p. 173ff ('The basic idea is that how an individual may be treated is determined, not by considering his group membership, but by considering his own particular characteristics'); McMahan (2005), p. 357 (noting that it is foundational to moral individualism that 'only intrinsic properties can be status-conferring'); May (2014); Cavalieri (2001), p. 76.

[81] Tanner (2006), p. 56f.

[82] See Cruft et al. (2015), p. 9 (noting that 'there does not seem to be a relevant empirical attribute that would apply to all and only human beings'); Fasel (2018), p. 477 (noting that 'there are likely no rights-grounding features that all and only human beings possess').

or indirectly morally significant in that it establishes the (real or fictional) possession of the human rights-relevant feature or capacity.

2.3.3.3 Neo-Dignitarian Accounts and the Retreat into Autopoietic Insulation

Some exceptionalist theorists—sometimes referred to as 'new dignitarians'[83]— refrain from relying on empirical claims about human nature, and instead invoke an unapologetically transcendent notion of human dignity as the foundation of human rights.[84] For example, Catherine Dupré states that human rights protection 'rests on the assumption that, as human beings, we are born with the unique quality of dignity that distinguishes us from other beings (primarily animals), justifying and explaining the special protection of our rights'.[85] Whereas dignity has long served as a basis for human rights,[86] the recent revival of (neo-)dignitarian justifications may be explained as a counter-reaction to the corrosive critiques levelled against—and as a way of circumventing the pitfalls of—other exceptionalist accounts whose rationalist justifications falter once empirical evidence is introduced into abstract human nature.[87] As both Raffael Fasel and Will Kymlicka have astutely noted, neo-dignitarians precisely reclaim dignity as a metaphysical vehicle for reinforcing and insulating the idea of human exceptionalism *against* such empirical interferences.[88]

Indeed, new dignitarians are quite outspoken about their reliance on human dignity as a means of preserving special human rank. For example, Thomas Williams submits that in a disenchanted world where the natural sciences 'tend ever more to emphasize the continuity between man and other creatures', human dignity

---

[83] See Kymlicka (2018), p. 768 (noting that new dignitarians 'make two core claims: (1) that protection of, or respect for, human dignity is the basis of human rights; and (2) that a core component of human dignity is our radical difference from, and superiority over, animals'); Fasel (2019a) (arguing that this 'new dignitarianism' is in fact old).

[84] See e.g. Waldron (2015); Kateb (2011).

[85] Dupré (2015), p. 28.

[86] See Fellmeth (2016), p. 51 (noting that 'One of the most often invoked bases for human rights is the concept of intrinsic human dignity'); dignity is prominently listed as a basis for human rights in the Universal Declaration of Human Rights preamble ('recognition of the inherent dignity ... of all members of the human family') and article 1 ('All human beings are born free and equal in dignity and rights'); see also McCrudden (2008) (noting that the UDHR was 'pivotal in popularizing the use of "dignity" or "human dignity" in human rights discourse').

[87] cf. Douzinas (2000), p. 96 (noting that 'Once the slightest empirical or historical material is introduced into abstract human nature ... human nature with its equality and dignity retreats rapidly').

[88] See Fasel (2019a), p. 532 (noting that '"new dignitarians" are united in their enlisting of the concept of human dignity for the purpose of countering what they perceive to be threats to the special moral and legal status of humanity'); Kymlicka (2018), p. 768ff (noting that for new dignitarians, dignity serves as 'the vehicle for supremacist theories').

'provides a sure confirmation that man is not mistaken when he sees himself as radically distinct from and superior to the rest of the created world.'[89] For George Kateb, talk of human dignity is directed against deflationary 'naturalist reductions' that 'picture humanity as just another animal species among other animal species' and 'unnecessarily tarnish human dignity by taking away commendable uniqueness from it.' According to Kateb, the 'core idea of human dignity is that on earth, humanity is the greatest type of being ... and that every member deserves to be treated in a manner consonant with the high worth of the species.'[90] Richard Cupp, one of the most ardent critics of animal rights, writes that it 'is not alarmist to note that inventing new rights for animals would make us view humans as less special and unique' and warns against 'the relaxation of human dignity protections' as a dangerous corollary of animal rights.[91]

While it is clear that this particular narrative of human dignity cultivates a form of 'species aristocratism'[92] and seeks to 're-inscribe species hierarchy at the heart of [human rights] theory',[93] it is far from clear what exactly human dignity is, why all and only humans have it, what is so special about it,[94] and, one might ask, what about animal dignity?[95] Resort to the question-begging concept of dignity tends to give rise to more problems than it solves.[96] Dignity is generally 'an extremely indeterminate and historically complex concept', and often serves as a placeholder for other rationality-based properties which are believed to be unique in humans.[97] Insofar as dignity is referenced in this way, dignitarian accounts will run into the

---

[89] Williams (2005), p. 207.
[90] Kateb (2011), p. 3f, 128.
[91] Cupp (2009), p. 77.
[92] See Rossello (2016); on human rights aristocracy, see Fasel (2019b), p. 79ff.
[93] Kymlicka (2018), p. 768.
[94] See e.g. Etinson (2020), p. 354 (noting that the idea of a special human dignity 'is a wonderful piece of self-flattery' but that 'Dignity can be shared across species').
[95] See e.g. Loder (2016); indeed, some legal orders have moved to recognize the dignity, or intrinsic value, of nonhuman animals. See, e.g., Swiss Federal Constitution article 120(2) ('dignity of living beings') and Swiss Animal Welfare Act article 1 ('protect the dignity ... of animals'). On this, see further Bolliger (2016); Bernet Kempers (2020).
[96] See Fasel (2018), p. 481 (aptly noting that 'invoking human dignity as a ground for human rights simply seems to protract the issue of finding a morally relevant ground for the possession of human rights. Human dignity may be the ground for human rights, but what, then, is the ground for human dignity?'); Singer (2009), p. 573 (noting that talk of special human dignity 'is really just a piece of rhetoric unless it is given some support. What is it about human beings that gives them moral worth and dignity?').
[97] See Besson (2018), p. 34f; Valentini (2017), p. 863 (noting that the conceptual link between human rights and dignity is 'uninformative at best and counter-productive at worst' in that it pushes human rights 'into deep metaphysical waters'. This is because the notion of dignity is opaque and 'often just a placeholder for whichever human attribute grounds human rights, with different philosophical traditions disagreeing on the relevant attribute'); but see Habermas (2010), p. 466 (arguing that the concept of human dignity is not merely 'a classificatory expression, an empty placeholder, as it were, that lumps a multiplicity of different phenomena together').

same problems as the rationalist accounts discussed above, and seem to switch one conception of exceptional human nature that struggles to be grounded in empirical reality for another.[98] To the extent, however, that human dignity is not used as a placeholder but invoked as an independent foundational value, it appears to function as a mystic and self-referential 'Tû-Tû'[99] concept that escapes the possibility of verification or falsification, because it is simply posited as an axiom.[100] While the axiomatic invocation of dignity may, as intended, immunize the dignitarian account against the sort of empirical and philosophical scrutiny it sets out to evade, this retreat into autopoietic insulation is precisely what removes it from the realm of dialectical reasoning. At this point, dignitarian accounts fail to meet the justificatory burden of human rights philosophy. Instead of offering a proper justification of human rights, they simply reassert an unshakable belief in human exceptionalism, essentially 'making human rights a matter of faith rather than of reason.'[101] This, then, is really just 'speciesism in nicer terms',[102] dressed up in a dignified guise. As such, neo-dignitarian human rights may very well be the last bastion—or the dying gasp—of old humanism and the ideology of human exceptionalism it seeks to conserve.

2.3.4 Against Human Rights Exceptionalism

Exceptionalist conceptions seek to ground *exclusive* human rights in *unique* human nature—a justificatory strategy that is bound to fail. Philosophers for many centuries have tried to spell out 'what all and only the featherless bipeds have in common, thereby explaining what is essential to being human.'[103] This ongoing search for the 'anthropological difference'—those significant features that are *unique* to humans and set them apart from all animals—appears increasingly futile.[104] Darwinian naturalism and the past decades of scientific advances and bioethical debate have incrementally worked to debunk the idea of human exceptionalism, as its empirical and metaphysical assumptions are 'increasingly and evidently anachronistic'.[105]

---

[98] See also Fasel (2018), p. 480ff.
[99] See Ross (1957); on dignity as a tû-tû concept, see Pietrzykowski (2021), p. 72.
[100] See Liao (2010), p. 161 (noting that dignity is not 'an attribute that one can empirically identify and assess').
[101] Besson (2018), p. 23.
[102] Singer (2009), p. 573.
[103] Rorty (1993), p. 114; Abbey (2017), p. 3 (noting the 'time-honored Western preoccupation with what distinguishes humans from animals'); Schulz and Raman (2020), p. 29f.
[104] See Glock (2012), p. 109 (further noting that 'there is nothing special about being special. *Every* biological species differs from *all* the others, i.e. has unique features').
[105] Pietrzykowski (2018), p. 40; Gearty (2009), p. 181 (noting a 'collapse of intellectual confidence in the specialness of the human' and 'decline in arguments for human uniqueness'); Weitzenfeld and Joy (2014), p. 7 (noting how modern science leads us to conclude 'just how untenable human

Although human exceptionalism has become an outdated and free-floating ideology sans empirical foundation,[106] it remains very much alive in philosophical and legal thinking. Yet, attempts by theorists to sustain, defend, or rehabilitate human exceptionalism do seem to involve 'increasingly contorted intellectual gymnastics'.[107] This is also true of human rights philosophy.[108] As has become clear, the claim that *all and only* human beings have human rights is 'in fact surprisingly difficult to defend',[109] and attempts at doing so ultimately lead to either conceding that not all humans are right-holders or adopting a speciesist position.[110] While strictly rationalist justifications of human rights may be logically consistent, they risk undermining the equal rights of all humans, because they rely on a highly gradualized cognitive capacity that not all humans possess. Generically rationalist and dignitarian justifications circumvent this problem by relying on exceptionalist fictions or axioms that ultimately amount to 'nothing more than the bald assertion of speciesism.'[111] Staunch defenders of exceptionalist human rights will, however, hardly be dissuaded by the prospect of being labelled 'speciesists'. Indeed, some authors have moved to simply embrace (the practical necessity of) speciesism for grounding human rights, and rely on biological humanness as an axiomatic precondition that defies the need for further philosophical justification.[112] In the end, what it

---

exceptionalism and the human-animal dichotomy is'); Rorty (1993), p. 120 (noting that 'Darwin argued most of the intellectuals out of the view that human beings contain a special added ingredient'); Miah (2008), p. 82 (noting that in the wake of Darwinian biology the 'barriers between animals and humans have now begun to collapse'); Taylor (2010), p. 233 (noting that 'scientific findings and philosophical debate are rendering human exceptionalism increasingly untenable intellectually').

[106] See Taylor (2010), p. 234 (noting that the 'doctrine of human exceptionalism expresses an objectively outmoded world-view').

[107] Donaldson and Kymlicka (2011), p. 29.

[108] See e.g. Fellmeth (2016), p. 53 ('Although so far no philosopher . . . has formulated a compelling case against animal rights, there is widespread opposition among many philosophers to animal rights as a concept. . . . after more than four decades of sustained and intense effort, the numerous opponents of animal rights have been able to offer no especially persuasive reason that humans should have all the intrinsic rights and animals should have none'); Goodkin (1987), p. 284f (noting that 'theorists have been unable to identify the "unique" worth and dignity of humans in a way which logically accords natural rights to humans but not to animals').

[109] Liao (2010), p. 160.

[110] See Fasel (2018), p. 474 (noting that such attempts 'have all encountered a similar problem: either *only but not all* human beings possess the relevant features, or *all but not only* human beings possess these features').

[111] Donaldson and Kymlicka (2011), p. 29.

[112] For example, Pollmann (2014), p. 127f, seems to suggest that, because all naturalistic accounts are bound to succumb to circular reasoning, we should simply embrace the argumentative circle of the human rights syllogism and posit from the outset that species membership is necessary and sufficient for having human rights (i.e. all and only humans have human rights by definition, not in virtue of some essential quality 'X'); for a principled moral defense of speciesism, see generally Cohen (2001), p. 62ff.

comes down to is a kind of 'decisionism'[113]—a deliberate decision to uphold human exceptionalism despite the preponderance of empirical and philosophical arguments against it.[114] This mindset is best expressed by Alan Dershowitz, who admits that 'we have made the somewhat arbitrary decision to single out our own species— every single member of it—for different and better treatment. Does this subject us to the charge of speciesism? Of course it does, and *we cannot justify it* except by the fact that in the world in which we live, *humans make the rules*'.[115]

While we may have arrived at a discursive deadlock as regards the critique or defence of human exceptionalism,[116] there is another, human rights-internal reason that should incline us to think that exceptionalist theories cannot retain their explanatory monopoly over human rights. Exceptionalist accounts are typically bound up with rationalist reductions of human nature, and single out *one* highly abstract feature (e.g. personhood, agency, autonomy) as the foundation of *all* human rights. This rationalist-foundational monism[117] has generally been criticized as too restrictive, because it does not only risk being under-inclusive as regards the class of human rights-holders, but also as regards the aspects of human nature that fall within the protective mandate of human rights.[118] The rationalist-monist mode of grounding human rights 'restricts the human rights-generative interests to those in freedom or normative agency', while ignoring other obvious sources of human protective needs, such as the capacity to feel pain and suffer.[119] As John Tasioulas illustrates, many core human rights, such as the right not to be tortured, protect human interests that are not necessarily or primarily reducible to a rationality-related value, but are more plausibly explained as protecting a 'plurality of human interests', among them the interest in avoiding 'excruciating pain'.[120] Agency is certainly an important factor in the configuration of many human rights, but surely not the *only* important aspect of human nature deserving of human rights protection. For this reason, if we ground human rights in human nature, it seems best to adopt a position of

---

[113] On decisionism and its critique, see Kymlicka (2018), p. 780; Rossello (2017); Fasel (2019b), p. 114ff.

[114] See also Weitzenfeld and Joy (2014), p. 6 (noting a 'dogmatic, irrational adherence to human exceptionalism despite the empirical evidence of a continuum and multitude of species capabilities'); Taylor (2010), p. 234 (noting that 'Human exceptionalism is not a statement of fact, but an assertion of domination').

[115] Dershowitz (2004), p. 198 (emphasis added).

[116] See Taylor (2010), p. 234 (noting that 'What we have here are different paradigms – incompatible understandings of reality – and there is no common language to bridge the gap').

[117] Exceptionalist accounts are monist to the extent that they identify one basic value that grounds human rights. On the distinction between monist and pluralist human rights accounts, see e.g. Griffin (2012), p. 10f; Fasel (2018), p. 472f.

[118] See generally Cruft et al. (2015), p. 12; Gilabert (2015), p. 204 (noting that the focus is 'not on the urgent interests that all (or most) humans have, but on the subset of them that only humans have. We will then be unable to refer to obviously important interests such as avoiding pain when justifying human rights. This is too restrictive').

[119] Tasioulas (2015), p. 63; see also Gilabert (2015), p. 203.

[120] See Tasioulas (2012a), p. 13.

foundational pluralism.[121] This allows for a range of essential human features (among them rationality-based as well as more primal or corporeal interests) to play a justifying role in *different* human rights.[122] Such a pluralistic or 'explanatorily promiscuous'[123] foundation promises to more realistically reflect the complex and heterogeneous nature of humans, rather than committing human rights to one particular 'radical nature'.[124] It is further able to accommodate humans not only as extraordinary rational beings, but also as ordinary bodily and emotional beings 'who, unlike the abstractions of moral philosophy, hurt, feel pain and suffer'.[125]

As the next section will argue, non-exceptionalist naturalistic theories offer such a pluralistic, and more plausible, human rights paradigm—one that is able to justify universal human rights of all (but perhaps not only) humans on more diverse grounds that are not premised on questionable rationalist assumptions about special human nature.

2.4 Non-Exceptionalist Conceptions of Human Rights and the Rise of New Humanism

2.4.1 Overview

The second, more junior family of essentialist naturalistic theories grounds human rights in a non-exceptionalist conception of *typical* human nature. Non-exceptionalist accounts rest on a more realistic and profane image of humans as physically, socially, and politically vulnerable beings that possess basic interests, needs, and capabilities which human rights are supposed to protect and foster. This shift 'from transcendental rationalism to a sensate, suffering, sentimental human

---

[121] See e.g. Waldron (2015), p. 120 (encouraging us to 'think pluralistically about rights' because 'human nature is multi-faceted'); Tasioulas (2015), p. 51 (advocating a 'flexible, many-faceted approach to the grounding of human rights, whereby more than one interest, or combination of interests, grounds the existence of any given right'); Besson (2018), p. 31f (noting that 'pluralistic approaches to the justification of human rights are more promising'); Nickel (2007), p. 53 (advocating a 'pluralistic justificatory framework').

[122] See Tasioulas (2012a), p. 26 (adopting a pluralistic view means that 'At the level of foundations, a plurality of values plays a role in grounding human rights'); it is generally questionable whether it makes sense to pinpoint *one* single foundation of *all* human rights. See e.g. Douzinas (2000), p. 4 (submitting that 'there can be no general theory of human rights') and Waldron (2015), p. 120 (noting that 'it is not necessary for there to be a single theory of humanity').

[123] Winston (2007), p. 297 (submitting that 'most human rights receive their justifications from a variety of sources' and that the 'human rights canon as a whole ... is justified holistically by ... multiple anchors as well as multiple interdependencies').

[124] Chartier (2010), p. 45f (noting that the 'conceptual price of denying that animals have moral rights seems to be commitment to the view that rights are grounded in radical natures that may entirely lack empirical manifestation').

[125] Douzinas (2000), p. 239.

2.4 Non-Exceptionalist Conceptions of Human Rights and the Rise of New Humanism

body' marks a clear departure from old humanism.[126] Indeed, many critical—especially feminist, disability, and vulnerability—scholars are vocal about replacing the traditional, abstract, disembodied rational agent as human right-holder with embodied 'real-life subjects' reflective of the 'lived realities of human subjects.'[127] The justifications advanced for human rights typically centre on simple human features or capacities that are commonly shared by all humans (and, incidentally, by many other animals).[128]

For example, human rights are often seen as protecting a plurality of especially important, *fundamental human interests*.[129] Others frame human rights as grounded in *basic needs*,[130] the fundamental conditions for a *minimally good life*,[131] or basic human *capabilities*.[132] Still others identify embodied *vulnerability*—the 'universal, inevitable, enduring aspect of the human condition'[133]—as basis for universal human rights.[134] Anna Grear calls to mind that it was the 'embodied nature of the human suffering that gave international human rights law its founding impulse',[135]

---

[126] See Golder (2016), p. 689f (further noting that this 'reworking of the foundations of human rights thus departs from the disembodied Kantian subject' and introduces 'the wounded, sensate, suffering body of humanity beseeching protection'); on the 'new humanistic discourse' that grounds human rights in corporeal vulnerability, needs, or capabilities, see Murphy (2011).

[127] Fineman (2008), p. 10, 12 (submitting that 'the "vulnerable subject" must replace the autonomous and independent subject asserted in the liberal tradition. Far more representative of actual lived experience and the human condition, the vulnerable subject should be at the center of our political and theoretical endeavors.' Ibid., p. 2); Grear (2007), p. 522 (noting that 'The unitary subject of law in liberal legal theory builds on ... an abstract, socially de-contextualised, hyper-rational, wilful individual systematically stripped of particularities, complexities and materiality.').

[128] See Fasel (2018), p. 476 (noting that accounts which advance a 'broad human rights grounding' will typically 'propose simple features or less demanding interpretations of more complex features').

[129] See e.g. Tasioulas (2015), p. 51, 70 (human rights 'are grounded in the universal interests of their holders', and there is an open-ended plurality of human rights-relevant interests); Besson (2018), p. 25 (noting that human rights 'protect fundamental human interests that all human beings have'); Edmundson (2012), p. 158 (noting that human rights 'recognize extraordinarily special, basic interests').

[130] See e.g. Renzo (2015); Brock (2005), p. 65f.

[131] See e.g. Liao (2015); Buchanan (2006), p. 153 (human rights as safeguarding the minimal benchmark of a 'decent or minimally good life'); Hare (1973), p. 140 (noting that human rights set and protect a normative standard for what we deem a minimally acceptable level of human existence. This standard is historically contingent 'as our conception of what is minimally acceptable changes and standards rise').

[132] See e.g. Nussbaum (2007), p. 21f (understanding human rights as 'entitlements to capabilities' that serve as a 'benchmark for a minimally decent human life'); Sen (2005); Vizard et al. (2011).

[133] Fineman (2008), p. 8.

[134] See e.g. Grear (2007), p. 541 (noting that the 'true basis of a universal, is the ontological given of our embodiment with its inherent vulnerability'); Cole (2016), p. 261 (vulnerability as 'shared, constitutive and connective feature of our existence that encompasses not merely susceptibility to harm but also receptivity to positive forms of intersubjectivity'); Turner (2006); Andorno (2016); Peroni and Timmer (2013); Marcos (2016).

[135] Grear (2007), p. 521, 539.

and submits that 'the protection of embodied beings' and 'the prevention of the suffering of the embodied human being' is at the heart of the human rights system.[136]

2.4.2 Incidental Exclusivity and Inherent Transspecies Inclusivity

While there is a broad diversity of non-exceptionalist naturalistic accounts, what these approaches have in common is that they do not conceptualize human nature in contradistinction to animals, but rather, identify core aspects of human existence regardless of whether such features are shared with other animals or not.[137] In fact, this family of naturalistic theories tends to be quite cognizant of the animal nature of humans[138] and of the evolutionary continuities between human and nonhuman animals. Even so, most of these human rights accounts are framed in humanist terms and are anthropocentric in that they, like old humanists, 'focus almost exclusively on the human species'[139] while being indifferent or inattentive to other animals. Unlike old humanism, however, this kind of new humanism[140] is not invested in the idea of human exceptionalism, and justifies human rights in a way that is merely inclusive of *all* humans without simultaneously encoding the demarcation from and exclusion of animals.[141] As a consequence, non-exceptionalist accounts remain conceptually agnostic about, or simply oblivious to, the incidental exclusion or potential inclusion of animals into the ambit of human rights protection.[142] It is this agnosticism towards the animal question that renders non-exceptionalist conceptions of human rights both *incidentally* (as opposed to

---

[136] Grear (2006), p. 195 (she points out that 'there is an inescapable emphasis on embodiment and the prevention of the suffering of the embodied human being. The right to life, to immunity from torture, to immunity from slavery, and a host of other rights in the lexicon of international human rights law ... focus on the protection of embodied beings. Such rights, in fact, make no conceptual sense without presupposing a vulnerable living body. ... this theme of embodiment is so central that it can be argued that it provides a kind of over-arching interpretive context').

[137] See e.g. Gilabert (2015), p. 203f (noting that 'when we identify important human interests, we look for normatively relevant general features of human beings without regard as to whether some of these features are also held by other beings, for example non-human animals'. He further notes that the 'relevant contrast when shaping our ideas of ... human rights is not between humans and other species, but between what belongs to all humans and what belongs to some by reference to special features such as race, class, and nationality.' Ibid., p. 206).

[138] cf. Ladwig (2014).

[139] Naffine (2012), p. 69.

[140] On new humanism, see Murphy (2011); Blau and Moncada (2009).

[141] See also Kymlicka (2018), p. 768 (noting that such accounts defend human rights 'in a way that does not rest on species hierarchy' and that is not 'essentially tied to the assertion of superiority over animals').

[142] See also Kymlicka (2018), p. 766f; in a similar vein, Vink (2020), p. 16 (noting an attitude of 'cavalier agnosticism' among political theorists who 'have simply never considered the option of

necessarily) *exclusive* yet *inherently* (albeit perhaps accidentally) *inclusive* of animals. Because the 'human' in human rights here serves as a placeholder for an essential human feature that *all but not only* humans share, non-exceptionalist accounts are over-inclusive or overshooting in that they lay the ground for potential animal rights along with grounding human rights.[143] Indeed, given the natural commonalities between humans and animals as regards possession of the human rights-grounding features (be they fundamental interests, basic needs, well-being, capabilities, or vulnerability), the standard justifications advanced for *human* rights quite readily extend to justifications of *animal* rights.[144]

Take, for example, the interest-based approach, which grounds human rights in fundamental human interests. Some of these interests, such as those requiring complex cognitive abilities or those concerning particular human institutions like marriage or religion, will presumably be purely *human* interests. Other, more basic and ubiquitous interests (deriving from humans' animal rather than rational nature)[145] are however widely shared by other sentient animals, such as the interest in avoiding pain, suffering, injuries and death, or in having food, shelter, and an adequate family and social life.[146] On a species-neutral reading, the interest-based account[147] of human rights can thus be seen as grounding corresponding animal rights, based on shared fundamental interests.[148] This holds true even of overtly

---

involving non-humans' or who regard 'animals as trivial, not worthy of serious attention, or irrelevant to political theory').

[143] On this overinclusiveness, see Fasel (2018), p. 474 et passim.

[144] See Kymlicka (2018), p. 770 (noting that virtually all of these concepts 'which we standardly use to discuss and defend human rights – interests, needs, well-being, capabilities, flourishing, vulnerability, subjectivity, care, justice – lead naturally to the recognition of animal rights, since animals are continuous with humans in all of these respects').

[145] See Korsgaard (2011), p. 108 (highlighting that 'the self for whom things can be naturally good or bad is not merely your rational self. It is also, or rather it is, your animal self').

[146] See e.g. Beauchamp (2011), p. 205 (noting that 'humans and many nonhumans share various interests that merit protection by rights. Some basic rights of humans and members of other species derive from conditions of vulnerability and potential harm').

[147] It is worth highlighting that the interest theory of rights (from which the interest-based conception of human rights derives) is generally accepting and inclusive of animals as (potential or actual) right-holders. See Stucki (2020), p. 542ff; Kurki (2019), pp. 62–65; Kramer (2001).

[148] That is, if a particular human right to X protects a fundamental interest X, and some animals (along with all humans) have a comparable interest in X, it would plausibly follow that the right to X is not just a human but also a potential animal right. See Fellmeth (2016), p. 53 ('Similar interests justify similar treatment ... If animals have an interest in living and being free from torture no different from that of human beings, then a strong case can be made ... for giving them corresponding rights'); Edmundson (2012), p. 158 (noting that 'talk of human rights serves the recognitional function of singling out extraordinarily important interests. Once it appears that some such particularly important interest is shared by nonhuman creatures – such as the interest in not being made to suffer gratuitous pain – it in no way derogates from the recognitional point to attribute the right to the nonhuman creature as well'); Beauchamp (2011), p. 205 ('to assume that all basic rights are for humans only is presumptive and prejudicial. Rights that are basic protect fundamental interests. Some interests – for example, in not being in pain, not suffering, having

anthropocentric conceptions such as the 'two-level pluralist account' formulated by John Tasioulas, which grounds human rights in 'both moral (equal human dignity) and prudential (universal human interests) considerations'.[149] While Tasioulas does not dispense with the unequivocally humanist notion of human dignity, his account is open to a species-neutral reformulation, as dignity here serves the conceptual function of marking moral status (i.e. having intrinsic or ultimate value), which is but a general interest-theoretical requirement for right-holding that animals can meet in virtue of their own dignity or inherent value.[150]

Along similar lines, if basic needs and capabilities, embodied vulnerability or the 'ubiquity of human misery and suffering'[151] are viewed as important grounds for human rights, it cannot go unnoticed that animals possess some of these human rights-generative features and might therefore also belong in the human rights-protective scheme. For example, Martha Nussbaum submits that the capabilities approach—even though initially developed with humans in mind—can be extended to other sentient animals.[152] According to her reformulation, basic animal rights should be determined based on a species-specific list of capabilities that affords all animals 'a shot at flourishing in their own way'.[153] The innate extensibility of human rights is perhaps clearest once we refocus on humans as vulnerable subjects whose embodiment 'carries with it the ever-present possibility of harm, injury, and misfortune'.[154] Animals—unlike corporations[155]—naturally share some of these

---

freedom of movement, having basic needs met, and the like – are not interests of humans only'); Bilchitz (2010), p. 277f (arguing that human rights should be 'inclusive of every individual with the fundamental interests necessary to be capable of benefiting from a particular right and needing its protection').

[149] Tasioulas (2015), p. 70. On his account, human dignity serves as the missing link between universal human interests and universal human rights, as it makes those interests normatively relevant. He describes this as 'a form of the interest-based theory which regards the interests in question as generative of human rights in crucial part because they are the interests of human beings who possess equal moral status: human dignity and universal human interests are equally fundamental grounds of human rights, characteristically bound together in their operation.' Ibid., p. 53f.

[150] The interest theory generally regards only those as right-holders whose interests are of 'ultimate value' (Raz (1986), p. 166, 177ff), i.e., who have 'moral status' (Kramer (2001), p. 33ff); Tasioulas (2015), p. 55, concedes this point when noting that 'the value of human dignity is one way, albeit not the only way, of satisfying this general condition for rights-bearing capacity'; on animals satisfying the moral status or inherent value criterion for right-holding, see generally Stucki (2020), p. 542f.

[151] Turner (2006), p. 34.

[152] For an application of the capabilities approach to animal rights, see Nussbaum (2005), p. 305ff (showing that the capabilities approach 'can be extended to provide a more adequate basis for animal entitlements'); Nussbaum (2011); Schinkel (2008).

[153] Nussbaum (2018), p. 11.

[154] Fineman (2008), p. 9.

[155] See Isiksel (2016), p. 332ff; Grear (2007), p. 542 (noting that 'corporations as disembodied jural entities do not share the foundational qualification for identification as a human rights beneficiary: embodied vulnerability').

fundamental vulnerabilities with humans.[156] Hence, if the embodied vulnerability of humans gives rise to universal human rights, and other animals are kindred vulnerable subjects, the vulnerability approach can be seen as co-justifying animal rights.[157]

All of this goes to show that with any given non-exceptionalist naturalistic account, the argument for transspecies inclusivity follows the same syllogistic logic: if animals have similar natural constitutions as human rights-holders, that is, to the extent that animals possess the rights-grounding natural qualities, a *human* right can be extended to a corresponding *animal* right.[158]

2.4.3 Human Rights Universalism Unbound

The decline of old humanism and the rise of new humanism is paralleled by a shift from an exclusive to an inclusive human rights paradigm. Non-exceptionalist conceptions of human rights drop the 'Herculean task' of finding a unique natural feature that (all and) *only* humans possess, and instead settle for more typical features that *all* (but not only) humans share.[159] In doing so, non-exceptionalist accounts put forward a more plausible reading of universality that signals simple inclusivity rather than exclusivity—one that takes 'being human' to be a sufficient but not necessarily a necessary condition for having human rights.[160] It is precisely due to its agnosticism or openness towards the nonhuman that new humanism has furnished a paradigm of radical, uncontainable inclusivity whose overshooting potential con-

---

[156] See Satz (2013), p. 176 (noting that 'Human and nonhuman animals share universal vulnerability to suffering with respect to certain basic capabilities'); Cole (2016), p. 263 (noting that 'Vulnerability is a condition of life, both human and nonhuman'); Grear (2013), p. 50 (vulnerability as 'fundamental, trans-species ontic commonality – a form of shared quintessential affectability as a condition or quality of creaturely existence itself').

[157] See e.g. Turner (2006), p. 37f (noting that 'Giving rights to animals may not undermine the vulnerability argument, because animal rights are not unlike the rights enjoyed by other agents ... who cannot directly and actively enforce their own rights'); Satz (2013), p. 176 (noting that animals are vulnerable to severe deprivations of their basic needs as well as 'uniquely vulnerable to exploitation'); Eisen (2018), p. 941 ff.

[158] See e.g. Goodkin (1987), p. 276; Beaudry (2016), p. 12.

[159] See Fasel (2018), p. 477 (succinctly noting that 'If identifying rights-grounding features that all and only human beings possess is such a Herculean task, we are well advised to drop the criterion that *only* human beings must possess these features. It may be sufficient ... to ground human rights in those features that *all* (but not only) human beings possess').

[160] See e.g. Buchanan (2011), p. 213f (noting that 'a plausible understanding of the claim that human rights are rights we have by virtue of our humanity does *not* imply that the concept of human rights is applicable only to human beings'); Gardner (2008), p. 5 (asking whether we are too restrictive 'by insisting that humanity be both a necessary *and* a sufficient condition of the possession of a human right? Wouldn't sufficiency suffice?').

tains the seeds for extending universal human rights beyond the human species.[161] This potential for transspecies universality is inherent and derives from the very justificatory logic of non-exceptionalist human rights.[162] On a justificatory level, then, many human rights are—or could very well be—animal rights.[163] In fact, all of this suggests that in a conceptual sense, human rights are not and may 'have never been only or wholly human.'[164]

Notwithstanding this inherent potential for transspecies inclusivity, it must be acknowledged that even the more expansive and inclusive human rights paradigm offered by new humanism remains ultimately humanist, albeit reflective of a humanism light or an 'inclusive humanism'.[165] While non-exceptionalist accounts provide plenty of conceptual space for integrating animals into the human rights framework, this process is somewhat predicated on the 'human-likeness' of animals. The operative logic is that human rights can be extended to animals because, and to the extent that, animals are like humans with regard to the relevant rights-grounding feature, and thus relies heavily on the natural similarities and 'empathetic proximity' between humans and animals.[166] This assimilationist or sameness approach, with its modified criterion of 'being human-like' (instead of 'being human'), has attracted the criticism of engaging in a 'human-like chauvinism' (instead of 'human chauvinism') that reinforces anthropocentric values.[167] Echoing second wave feminist critiques, Catharine MacKinnon asks us: 'Why should animals have to measure up

---

[161] See also Donaldson and Kymlicka (2011), p. 24 (noting that the 'universalizing impulse of human rights is to extend basic protections across boundaries of physical, mental, and cultural difference, so why should this impulse stop at the boundary of the human species?').

[162] This point was notably made by Cavalieri (2001), p. 139. Cavalieri contends that 'on the basis of the very doctrine that establishes them, human rights are not *human*.' She continues to elaborate that 'the will to secure equal fundamental rights to all human beings, including the non-paradigmatic ones, has implied that the characteristics appealed to in order to justify the ascription of such rights ... lie at a cognitive-emotive level accessible to a large number of nonhuman animals.' She concludes that 'not only is there nothing in the doctrine of human rights to motivate the reference to our species ... but it is the same justificatory argument underlying it that drives us toward the attribution of human rights to members of species other than our own.'

[163] See e.g. Gilabert (2015), p. 205 ('Surely there are *animal* rights that partly overlap with *human* rights').

[164] Hunt (2011), p. 226 (further noting that 'there is nothing but the anthropomorphic disfiguration of ideology to prevent us from affirming that nonhuman entities are subjects of rights.' Ibid, p. 242).

[165] Pietrzykowski (2018), p. 102ff (arguing that 'what seems necessary is not rejecting juridical humanism as such, but rather eliminating its present exclusive, or exceptionalist, thread').

[166] See Redgwell (1996), p. 77; Tribe (1974), p. 1343.

[167] See Sapontzis (1993), p. 271; for a critique of sameness, similarity, or assimilationist approaches, see generally Bryant (2007); Deckha (2012) (calling for 'respect for embodied difference rather than partial sameness', ibid., p. 234); Nussbaum (2018), p. 3ff (questioning the 'So Like Us' approach); Beaudry (2016), p. 12ff; Jenkins and Stanescu (2014), p. 76 (submitting that 'Anthropocentric privilege defines the criteria for inclusion in the moral community through the glorification of human-centric capacities').

2.4 Non-Exceptionalist Conceptions of Human Rights and the Rise of New Humanism

to humans' standards for humanity before their existence counts?'[168] This criticism seems particularly pertinent with regard to certain practical attempts to extend autonomy-based human rights to animals,[169] which tend to focus on cognitively human-like animals such as great apes (hominids)—humans' next of kin.[170] Presumably, on a rationalist approach, only the most *humanoid* animals—as quasi-humans, 'adoptive humans',[171] or 'honorary humans'[172]—would be allowed entry into the exclusive club of human(oid) rights.[173]

However, the 'largely cognition-based case for hominid rights' is somewhat different from 'the largely sentience-based case' for general animal rights.[174] The fact that animals are sentient beings is not relevant merely because they are like humans in this respect. Rather, there are good reasons to think that sentience is a natural quality that has intrinsic moral and rights-generative significance.[175] For example, Sue Donaldson and Will Kymlicka submit that 'Being an "I"—a being who experiences—represents a particular kind of vulnerability, calling for a particular form of protection ... in the form of inviolable rights.'[176] Non-exceptionalist conceptions that take into account the manifold needs, interests, and vulnerabilities arising from the animal nature of humans *as* sentient beings thus seem better

---

[168] MacKinnon (2005), p. 267 ('That women are like men and animals are like people is thought to establish their existential equality, hence their right to rights ... the issue is, is this the right question? ... It is not that women and animals do not have these qualities. It is why animals should have to be like people to be let alone by them, to be free of the predations and exploitations and atrocities people inflict on them, or to be protected from them. Animals don't exist for humans any more than women exist for men'); see also Offor (2020).

[169] The most prominent example here is the 'practical autonomy' approach developed by Wise (2002) and strategically litigated in courts by the Nonhuman Rights Project. On the Nonhuman Rights Project, see e.g. Wise (2010); Fernandez (2018).

[170] For strategic purposes, some animal rights practitioners direct their focus on great apes, because these nonhuman hominids naturally show close genetic, morphological, cognitive, and emotional similarities with human hominids and are thus believed to be the most plausible (the most *human-like*) candidates for nonhuman human rights – or '*hominid rights*'. On such hominid rights, see Taylor (2001) (claiming that 'Hominid rights are more likely to win acceptance if they are seen as applying only to *beings like us*', ibid., p. 39 [emphasis added]); Andrews et al. (2018).

[171] Deckha (2012), p. 233 (noting that 'the humanist paradigm does not shift').

[172] Fox (2004), p. 480.

[173] See also MacKinnon (2005), p. 325 (noting that on this 'like us' model animal rights 'are poised to develop first for a tiny elite'); Donaldson and Kymlicka (2007), p. 194 (noting that this strategy 'does not disrupt the human-animal hierarchy').

[174] Taylor (2001), p. 41.

[175] See e.g. Nussbaum (2018), p. 14 (noting that 'sentience is an important boundary in the world of nature, a baseline requirement of ethical considerability ... Pain is the great evil'); Singer (1995), p. 8f (proposing that 'the limit of sentience (using the terms as a convenient if not strictly accurate shorthand for the capacity to suffer and/or experience enjoyment) is the only defensible boundary of concern for the interests of others'); Singer (2011), p. 123 (further noting that 'the boundary of sentience ... is not a morally arbitrary boundary in the way that the boundaries of race or species are arbitrary'); see also Peters (2021), p. 502ff.

[176] Donaldson and Kymlicka (2011), p. 33.

equipped to also accommodate the specific interests, needs, and vulnerabilities of animals as sentient beings.[177]

In the end, although human rights are originally anthropocentric and may retain a certain degree of anthropocentrism even under new humanism, the inclusion of animals can be argued in a conceptually consistent and normatively meaningful manner. Yet, as Kelly Oliver stresses, 'although rights may be better than no rights, they also do not go far enough in addressing the structural and ideological issues that made them necessary in the first place.'[178] To appreciate the historical and social conditions that create a practical need for animal rights, we need a political perspective beyond human rights naturalism.

References

Abbey R (2017) Closer kinships: Rortyan resources for animal rights. Contemp Polit Theory 16:1–18
Andorno R (2016) Is vulnerability the Foundation of Human Rights? In: Masferrer A, García-Sánchez E (eds) Human dignity of the vulnerable in the age of rights. Springer, Cham, pp 257–272
Andrews K et al (2018) Chimpanzee rights: the philosopher's brief. Routledge, London
Beauchamp TL (2011) Rights theory and animal rights. In: Beauchamp TL, Frey RG (eds) Oxford handbook of animal ethics. Oxford University Press, Oxford, pp 198–227
Beaudry JS (2016) From autonomy to habeas corpus: animal rights activists take the parameters of legal personhood to court. Global J Anim Law 1(2016):3–35
Beitz CR (2004) Human rights and the law of peoples. In: Chatterjee DK (ed) The ethics of assistance: morality and the distant needy. Cambridge University Press, Cambridge, pp 193–214
Beitz CR (2009) The idea of human rights. Oxford University Press, Oxford
Benton T (1988) Humanism = Speciesism: Marx on humans and animals. Radic Philos 50:4–18
Bernet Kempers E (2020) Animal dignity and the law: potential, problems and possible implications. Liverpool Law Rev 41:173–199
Besson S (2018) Justifications. In: Moeckli D, Shah S, Sivakumaran S (eds) International human rights law, 3rd edn. Oxford University Press, Oxford, pp 22–40
Bilchitz D (2009) Moving beyond arbitrariness: the legal personhood and dignity of non-human animals. South Afr J Human Rights 25:38–72
Bilchitz D (2010) Does transformative constitutionalism require the recognition of animal rights? South Afr Public Law 25:267–300
Blau J, Moncada A (2009) The new humanism: beyond modernity and postmodernity. In: Morgan R, Turner BS (eds) Interpreting human rights: social science perspectives. Routledge, London, pp 141–156
Bolliger G (2016) Legal protection of animal dignity in Switzerland: status quo and future perspectives. Anim Law Rev 22:311–395
Brock G (2005) Needs and global justice. Royal Inst Philosophy Suppl 57:51–72
Bryant TL (2007) Similarity or difference as a basis for justice: must animals be like humans to be legally protected from humans? Law Contemp Probl 70:207–254

---

[177] See also MacKinnon (2005), p. 325 (noting that 'Predicating animal rights on the ability to suffer is less likely to fall into this trap, as it leads more directly to a strategy for all').
[178] Oliver (2008), p. 218.

References

Buchanan A (2006) Taking the human out of human rights. In: Martin R, Reidy DA (eds) Rawls's law of peoples: a realistic utopia? Blackwell, Malden, pp 150–168
Buchanan A (2011) Beyond humanity? The ethics of biomedical enhancement. Oxford University Press, Oxford
Cavalieri P (2001) The animal question: why nonhuman animals deserve human rights. Oxford University Press, Oxford
Chartier G (2010) Natural law and animal rights. Canadian J Law Jurisprud 23:33–46
Cochrane A (2013) From human rights to sentient rights. Crit Rev Int Soc Pol Phil 16:655–675
Cohen C (2001) In defense of the use of animals. In: Cohen C, Regan T (eds) The animal rights debate. Rowman & Littlefield, Lanham
Cole A (2016) All of us are vulnerable, but some are more vulnerable than others: the political ambiguity of vulnerability studies, an ambivalent critique. Crit Horiz 17:260–277
Corbey R (2013) 'Race' and species in the post-world war II United Nations discourse on human rights. In: Corbey R, Lanjouw A (eds) The politics of species: reshaping our relationships with other animals. Cambridge University Press, Cambridge, pp 67–76
Costello K, Hodson G (2014) Explaining dehumanization among children: the interspecies model of prejudice. Br J Soc Psychol 53:175–197
Cruft R, Liao SM, Renzo M (2015) The philosophical foundations of human rights: an overview. In: Cruft R, Liao SM, Renzo M (eds) Philosophical foundations of human rights. Oxford University Press, Oxford, pp 1–41
Cupp RL (2009) Moving beyond animal rights: a legal/contractualist critique. San Diego Law Rev 46:27–84
D'Amato A, Chopra SK (1991) Whales: their emerging right to life. Am J Int Law 85:21–62
Deckha M (2012) Critical animal studies and animal law. Anim Law 18:207–236
Dershowitz A (2004) Rights from wrongs: a secular theory of the origins of rights. Basic Books, New York
Dombrowski DA (1997) Babies and beasts: the argument from marginal cases. University of Illinois Press, Champaign
Donaldson S, Kymlicka W (2007) The moral ark. Queen's Quarterly 114:187–205
Donaldson S, Kymlicka W (2011) Zoopolis: a political theory of animal rights. Oxford University Press, Oxford
Donnelly J (2013) Universal human rights in theory and practice, 3rd edn. Cornell University Press, Ithaca
Douzinas C (2000) The end of human rights: critical legal thought at the turn of the century. Hart, Oxford
Dupré C (2015) The age of dignity: human rights and constitutionalism in Europe. Hart, Oxford
Eckersley R (1998) Beyond human racism. Environ Values 7:165–182
Edmundson WA (2012) An introduction to rights, 2nd edn. Cambridge University Press, Cambridge
Eisen J (2018) Animals in the constitutional state. Int J Const Law 15:909–954
Etinson A (2020) What's so special about human dignity? Philos Public Aff 48:353–381
Fasel R (2019a) The old 'new' dignitarianism. Res Publica 25:531–552
Fasel RN (2018) 'Simply in virtue of being human'? A critical appraisal of a human rights commonplace. Jurisprudence 9:461–485
Fasel RN (2019b) More equal than others: animals in the age of human rights aristocracy, PhD thesis. University of Cambridge
Feinberg J (1973) Social philosophy. Prentice-Hall, Englewood Cliffs
Feinberg J, Baum Levenbook B (1993) Abortion. In: Regan T (ed) Matters of life and death: new introductory essays in moral philosophy, 3rd edn. McGraw-Hill, New York, pp 195–234
Fellmeth AX (2016) Paradigms of international human rights law. Oxford University Press, Oxford
Fernandez A (2018) Legal history and rights for nonhuman animals: an interview with Steven M. Wise. Dalhousie Law J 41:197–218

Fineman MA (2008) The vulnerable subject: anchoring equality in the human condition. Yale J Law Fem 20:1–23
Fjellstrom R (2002) Specifying speciesism. Environ Values 11:63–74
Fox M (2004) Re-thinking kinship: Law's construction of the animal body. Curr Leg Probl 57:469–493
Frey RG (1988) Moral standing, the value of lives, and speciesism. Between Spec 4:191–201
Gardner J (2008) 'Simply in virtue of being human': the whos and whys of human rights. J Ethics Soc Philosophy 2(2):1–23. https://doi.org/10.26556/jesp.v2i2.23
Gearty C (2009) Is human rights Speciesist? In: Linzey A (ed) The link between animal abuse and human violence. Sussex Academic Press, Brighton, pp 175–183
Gearty C (2010) Do human rights help or hinder environmental protection? J Human Rights Environ 1:7–22
Gewirth A (1982a) Introduction. In: Gewirth A (ed) Human rights: essays on justification and applications. University of Chicago Press, Chicago, pp 1–38
Gewirth A (1982b) The basis and content of human rights. In: Gewirth A (ed) Human rights: essays on justification and applications. University of Chicago Press, Chicago, pp 41–78
Gilabert P (2015) Human rights, human dignity, and power. In: Cruft R, Liao SM, Renzo M (eds) Philosophical foundations of human rights. Oxford University Press, Oxford, pp 196–213
Glock HJ (2012) The anthropological difference: what can philosophers do to identify the differences between human and non-human animals? Royal Inst Philosophy Suppl 70:105–131
Golder B (2016) Theorizing human rights. In: Orford A, Hoffmann F (eds) Oxford handbook of the theory of international law. Oxford University Press, Oxford, pp 684–700
Goodkin SL (1987) The evolution of animal rights. Columbia Human Rights Law Rev 18:259–288
Grear A (2006) Human rights – human bodies? Some reflections on corporate human rights distortion, the legal subject, embodiment and human rights theory. Law Critique 17:171–199
Grear A (2007) Challenging corporate 'humanity': legal disembodiment, embodiment and human rights. Hum Rights Law Rev 7:511–543
Grear A (2011) The vulnerable living order: human rights and the environment in a critical and philosophical perspective. J Human Rights Environ 2:23–44
Grear A (2013) Vulnerability, advanced global capitalism and co-symptomatic injustice: locating the vulnerable subject. In: Fineman MA, Grear A (eds) Vulnerability: reflections on a new ethical foundation for law and Politics. Ashgate, Farnham, pp 41–60
Griffin J (2001) Discrepancies between the best philosophical account of human rights and the international law of human rights. Proc Aristot Soc 101:1–28
Griffin J (2008) On human rights. Oxford University Press, Oxford
Griffin J (2010) Human rights and the autonomy of international law. In: Besson S, Tasioulas J (eds) The philosophy of international law. Oxford University Press, Oxford, pp 339–355
Griffin J (2012) Human rights: questions of aim and approach. In: Ernst G, Heilinger JC (eds) The philosophy of human rights: contemporary controversies. De Gruyter, Berlin, pp 3–16
Gruen L (2011) Ethics and animals: an introduction. Cambridge University Press, Cambridge
Habermas J (2010) The concept of human dignity and the realistic utopia of human rights. Metaphilosophy 41:464–480
Hare W (1973) Human rights, rhetoric and idle uses. J Thought 8:138–146
Haslam N (2006) Dehumanization: an integrative review. Personal Soc Psychol Rev 10:252–264
Haslam N (2014) What is dehumanization? In: Bain PG, Vaes J, Leyens JP (eds) Humanness and dehumanization. Routledge, New York/London, pp 34–48
Horkheimer M, Adorno TW (2002) Dialectic of Enlightenment (trans: Jephcott E, ed: Schmid Noerr G). Stanford University Press, Stanford
Horta O (2014) The scope of the argument from species overlap. J Appl Philos 31:142–154
Hunt A (2011) The rights of the infinite. Qui Parle 19:223–251
Isiksel T (2016) The rights of man and the rights of the man-made: corporations and human rights. Hum Rights Q 38:294–349

References

Jenkins S, Stanescu V (2014) One Struggle. In: Nocella AJ II, Sorenson J, Socha K, Matsuoka A (eds) Defining critical animal studies: an intersectional social justice approach for liberation. Peter Lang, New York, pp 74–85

Jowitt J (2020) Legal rights for animals: aspiration or logical necessity? J Human Rights Environ 11:173–198

Kateb G (2011) Human dignity. Harvard University Press, Cambridge

Korsgaard (2011) Interacting with animals: a Kantian account. In: Beauchamp TL, Frey RG (eds) Oxford handbook of animal ethics. Oxford University Press, Oxford, pp 91–118

Kramer MH (2001) Do animals and dead people have legal rights? Canadian J Law Jurisprud 14:29–54

Kurki VAJ (2019) A theory of legal personhood. Oxford University Press, Oxford

Kymlicka W (2018) Human rights without human supremacism. Can J Philos 48:763–792

Ladwig B (2014) Human rights and human animals. In: Albers M, Hoffmann T, Reinhardt J (eds) Human rights and human nature. Springer, Dordrecht, pp 23–42

LaFollette H, Shanks N (1996) The origin of speciesism. Philosophy 71:41–61

Lamont C (1997) The philosophy of humanism, 8th edn. Humanist Press, Amherst

Liao SM (2010) The basis of human moral status. J Moral Philos 7:159–179

Liao SM (2012) The genetic account of moral status: a defense. J Moral Philos 9:265–277

Liao SM (2015) Human rights as fundamental conditions for a good life. In: Cruft R, Liao SM, Renzo M (eds) Philosophical foundations of human rights. Oxford University Press, Oxford, pp 79–100

Loder RE (2016) Animal dignity. Anim Law Rev 23:1–64

MacDonald M (1984) Natural rights. In: Waldron J (ed) Theories of rights. Oxford University Press, Oxford, pp 21–40

MacKinnon CA (2000) Points against postmodernism. Chicago-Kent Law Rev 75:687–712

MacKinnon CA (2005) Of mice and men: a feminist fragment on animal rights. In: Sunstein CR, Nussbaum MC (eds) Animal rights: current debates and new directions. Oxford University Press, Oxford, pp 263–276

Marcos A (2016) Vulnerability as a part of human nature. In: Masferrer A, García-Sánchez E (eds) Human dignity of the vulnerable in the age of rights. Springer, Cham, pp 29–44

Maritain J (2011) Christianity and democracy and the rights of man and natural law (trans: Anson DC). Ignatius Press, San Francisco

Masferrer A, García-Sánchez E (2016) Vulnerability and human dignity in the age of rights. In: Masferrer A, García-Sánchez E (eds) Human dignity of the vulnerable in the age of rights. Springer, Cham, pp 1–28

May T (2014) Moral individualism, moral Relationalism, and obligations to non-human animals. J Appl Philos 31:155–168

McCloskey HJ (1965) Rights. Philosophical Q 15:115–127

McCrudden C (2008) Human dignity and judicial interpretation of human rights. Eur J Int Law 19:655–724

McMahan J (2002) The ethics of killing: problems at the margins of life. Oxford University Press, Oxford

McMahan J (2005) Our fellow creatures. J Ethics 9:353–380

Miah A (2008) A critical history of posthumanism. In: Gordijn B, Chadwick R (eds) Medical enhancement and posthumanity. Springer, Heidelberg, pp 71–94

Miller D (2015) Joseph Raz on human rights. In: Cruft R, Liao SM, Renzo M (eds) Philosophical foundations of human rights. Oxford University Press, Oxford, pp 232–243

Morsink J (1999) The universal declaration of human rights: origins, drafting, and intent. University of Pennsylvania Press, Philadelphia

Murphy AV (2011) Corporeal vulnerability and the new humanism. Hypatia 26:575–590

Naffine N (2012) Legal personality and the natural world: on the persistence of the human measure of value. J Human Rights Environ 3:68–83

Nickel JW (2007) Making sense of human rights, 2nd edn. Blackwell, Malden

Nino CS (1991) The ethics of human rights. Clarendon Press, Oxford
Nobis N (2004) Carl Cohen's 'kind' arguments *for* animal rights and *against* human rights. J Appl Philos 21:43–59
Nussbaum M (2007) Human rights and human capabilities. Harv Human Rights J 20:21–24
Nussbaum M (2011) The capabilities approach and animal entitlements. In: Beauchamp TL, Frey RG (eds) Oxford handbook of animal ethics. Oxford University Press, Oxford, pp 228–251
Nussbaum MC (2005) Beyond 'Compassion and Humanity': justice for nonhuman animals. In: Sunstein CR, Nussbaum MC (eds) Animal rights: current debates and new directions. Oxford University Press, Oxford, pp 299–320
Nussbaum MC (2018) Working with and for animals: getting the theoretical framework right. J Human Dev Capabil 19:2–18
Offor I (2020) Second wave animal ethics and (global) animal law: a view from the margins. J Human Rights Environ 11:268–296
Ohlin JD (2005) Is the concept of the person necessary for human rights? Columbia Law Rev 105:209–249
Oliver K (2008) What is wrong with (animal) rights? J Specul Philos 22:214–224
Patterson C (2002) Eternal Treblinka: our treatment of animals and the holocaust. Lantern Books, New York
Peroni L, Timmer A (2013) Vulnerable groups: the promise of an emerging concept in European human rights convention law. Int J Const Law 11:1056–1085
Perrett RW (2000) Taking life and the argument from potentiality. Midwest Stud Philosophy 24:186–197
Peters A (2021) Animals in international law. Pocketbooks of the Hague Academy of international law. Brill/Nijhoff, Leiden/Boston
Pietrzykowski T (2017) The idea of non-personal subjects of law. In: Kurki VAJ, Pietrzykowski T (eds) Legal personhood: animals, artificial intelligence and the unborn. Springer, Cham, pp 49–67
Pietrzykowski T (2018) Personhood beyond humanism: animals, chimeras, autonomous agents and the law. Springer, Cham
Pietrzykowski T (2021) Against dignity: an argument for a non-metaphysical foundation of animal law. Archiwum Filozofii Prawa i Filozofii Społecznej 2021(2):69–82
Pollmann A (2014) Human rights beyond naturalism. In: Albers M, Hoffmann T, Reinhardt J (eds) Human rights and human nature. Springer, Dordrecht, pp 121–136
Quinn G, Arstein-Kerslake A (2012) Restoring the 'human' in 'human rights': personhood and doctrinal innovation in the UN disability convention. In: Gearty C, Douzinas C (eds) The Cambridge companion to human rights law. Cambridge University Press, Cambridge, pp 36–55
Rachels J (1990) Created from animals: the moral implications of Darwinism. Oxford University Press, Oxford
Raz J (1986) The morality of freedom. Clarendon Press, Oxford
Raz J (2010) Human rights without foundations. In: Besson S, Tasioulas J (eds) The philosophy of international law. Oxford University Press, Oxford, pp 321–337
Redgwell C (1996) Life, the universe and everything: a critique of anthropocentric rights. In: Boyle AE, Anderson MR (eds) Human rights approaches to environmental protection. Clarendon Press, Oxford, pp 71–87
Renzo M (2015) Human needs, human rights. In: Cruft R, Liao SM, Renzo M (eds) Philosophical foundations of human rights. Oxford University Press, Oxford, pp 570–587
Rorty R (1993) Human rights, rationality, and sentimentality. In: Shute S, Hurley S (eds) On human rights: the Oxford amnesty lectures. Basic Books, New York, pp 111–134
Ross A (1957) Tû-Tû. Harv Law Rev 70:812–825
Rossello D (2016) All in the (human) family? Species aristocratism in the return of human dignity. Political Theory 45:749–771
Rossello DH (2017) 'To be human, nonetheless, remains a decision': humanism as decisionism in contemporary critical political theory. Contemp Polit Theory 16:439–458

References

Rothhaar M (2014) Species, potentiality and their manipulation. In: Albers M, Hoffmann T, Reinhardt J (eds) Human rights and human nature. Springer, Dordrecht, pp 173–183

Routley R, Routley V (1979) Against the inevitability of human chauvinism. In: Goodpaster KE, Sayre KM (eds) Ethics and problems of the 21st century. University of Notre Dame Press, Notre Dame, pp 36–59

Sapontzis SF (1993) Aping persons – pro and con. In: Cavalieri P, Singer P (eds) The great ape project: equality beyond humanity. St. Martin's Griffin, New York, pp 269–277

Satz AB (2013) Animals as vulnerable subjects: beyond interest-convergence, hierarchy, and property. In: Fineman MA, Grear A (eds) Vulnerability: reflections on a new ethical foundation for law and Politics. Ashgate, Farnham, pp 171–197

Schinkel A (2008) Martha Nussbaum on animal rights. Ethics Environ 13:41–69

Schulz WF, Raman S (2020) The coming good society: why new realities demand new rights. Harvard University Press, Cambridge

Sen A (2005) Human rights and capabilities. J Hum Dev 6:151–166

Singer P (1995) Animal liberation, 2nd edn. Pimlico, London

Singer P (2009) Speciesism and moral status. Metaphilosophy 40:567–581

Singer P (2011) The expanding circle: ethics, evolution, and moral progress (with a new preface and afterword). Princeton University Press, Princeton

Stone CD (1972) Should trees have standing? Toward legal rights for natural objects. South Calif Law Rev 45:450–501

Stucki S (2020) Towards a theory of legal animal rights: simple and fundamental rights. Oxf J Leg Stud 40:533–560

Tanner J (2006) Marginal humans, the argument from kinds and the similarity argument. Facta Universitatis: Ser Philosophy Sociol Psychol 5:47–63

Tanner JK (2009) The argument from marginal cases and the slippery slope objection. Environ Values 18:51–66

Tasioulas J (2012a) Towards a philosophy of human rights. Curr Leg Probl 65:1–30

Tasioulas J (2012b) On the nature of human rights. In: Ernst G, Heilinger JC (eds) The philosophy of human rights: contemporary controversies. De Gruyter, Berlin/Boston, pp 17–59

Tasioulas J (2015) On the foundations of human rights. In: Cruft R, Liao SM, Renzo M (eds) Philosophical foundations of human rights. Oxford University Press, Oxford, pp 45–70

Taylor A (2010) Review of Wesley J Smith's a rat is a pig is a dog is a boy: the human cost of the animal rights movement. Between Species 10:223–236

Taylor R (2001) A step at a time: New Zealand's Progress toward hominid rights. Animal Law 7:35–43

Tooley M (2009) Abortion: why a liberal view is correct. In: Tooley M, Wolf-Devine C, Devine P, Jaggar AM (eds) Abortion: three perspectives. Oxford University Press, New York, pp 3–64

Tribe LH (1974) Ways not to think about plastic trees: new foundations for environmental law. Yale Law J 83:1315–1348

Turner BS (2006) Vulnerability and human rights. Penn State University Press, University Park

Valentini L (2017) Dignity and human rights: a reconceptualisation. Oxf J Leg Stud 37:862–885

van Duffel S (2013) Moral philosophy. In: Shelton D (ed) Oxford handbook of international human rights law. Oxford University Press, Oxford, pp 32–53

Vink J (2020) The open society and its animals. Palgrave Macmillan/Springer, Cham

Vizard P, Fukuda-Parr S, Elson D (2011) Introduction: the capability approach and human rights. J Human Dev Capabil 12:1–22

Waldron J (2015) Is dignity the foundation of human rights? In: Cruft R, Liao SM, Renzo M (eds) Philosophical foundations of human rights. Oxford University Press, Oxford, pp 117–137

Weitzenfeld A, Joy M (2014) An overview of anthropocentrism, humanism, and speciesism in critical animal theory. In: Nocella AJ II, Sorenson J, Socha K, Matsuoka A (eds) Defining critical animal studies: an intersectional social justice approach for liberation. Peter Lang, New York, pp 3–27

Wellman C (2011) The moral dimensions of human rights. Oxford University Press, Oxford

Williams TD (2005) Who is my neighbor? Personalism and the foundations of human rights. Catholic University of America Press, Washington DC

Wills J (2020) Animal rights, legal personhood and cognitive capacity: addressing 'levelling-down' concerns. J Human Rights Environ 11:199–223

Winston M (2007) Human rights as moral rebellion and social construction. J Human Rights 6:279–305

Wise SM (2002) Drawing the line: science and the case for animal rights. Basic Books, New York

Wise SM (2010) Legal personhood and the nonhuman rights project. Anim Law Rev 17:1–12

Open Access This chapter is licensed under the terms of the Creative Commons Attribution 4.0 International License (http://creativecommons.org/licenses/by/4.0/), which permits use, sharing, adaptation, distribution and reproduction in any medium or format, as long as you give appropriate credit to the original author(s) and the source, provide a link to the Creative Commons license and indicate if changes were made.

The images or other third party material in this chapter are included in the chapter's Creative Commons license, unless indicated otherwise in a credit line to the material. If material is not included in the chapter's Creative Commons license and your intended use is not permitted by statutory regulation or exceeds the permitted use, you will need to obtain permission directly from the copyright holder.

Chapter 3
Political Conceptions of Human and Animal Rights: Principled and Prudential Reasons

> The emancipation of men will bring with it another and still wider emancipation – of animals. *Salt (1894), p. 94.*

The preceding chapter has argued that animals *could* have (some) human rights. Granted that the proposition of human rights for animals is conceptually plausible on naturalistic grounds, the question remains whether it is politically desirable on practical grounds. Would the inclusion of animals under the human rights framework be a good thing? Through the lens of political conceptions, this chapter explores a range of practical reasons why animals *should* be afforded human rights. I will argue that the extension of human rights to animals is warranted both for *principled* or ethical reasons (as a matter of justice for animals) and for *prudential* or instrumental reasons (as a means of better safeguarding human rights). In short, human rights are good for animals and animal rights are good for humans.

3.1 Human Rights Denaturalized: Constructing Rights on Practical Grounds

Almost 30 years ago, Richard Rorty proclaimed that 'human rights foundationalism is *outmoded*'.[1] Today, political conceptions of human rights are the main challenger to the orthodoxy of naturalistic conceptions.[2] In sharp contrast to the latter, political accounts refrain from relying on metaphysical and ahistorical assumptions about an abstract and intransient human nature as the philosophical foundation for human rights.[3] Paradigmatically, Morton Winston states that the belief in universal human

---

[1] Rorty (1993), p. 116; 'human rights foundationalism' denotes those conceptions which seek to isolate ahistorical, rationalist, transcendent grounds for human rights. See Golder (2016), p. 686.

[2] See e.g. Beitz (2004), p. 196 (contrasting the 'orthodox' view with 'practical' conceptions of human rights).

[3] See Rawls (1993), p. 56f (universal human rights 'do not depend on any particular comprehensive moral doctrine or philosophical conception of human nature' as these tend to be reflective of a

rights does not need a justification based on 'speculative philosophical conceptions of human nature'—a *pragmatic* justification will do.[4] Such 'alternative justificatory strategies' give *practical reasons* as to why a society should adopt and respect human rights.[5] Under the political conception, human rights are 'the product of human civilization and not nature',[6] and emerge from and evolve with social practice.[7] Political, practical, or functionalist accounts thus understand human rights in terms of their institutional and *practical functions*, considered in their concrete historical and socio-political context.

In a narrow sense, political conceptions such as the ones advanced by John Rawls,[8] Charles Beitz,[9] and Joseph Raz[10] explain human rights in terms of their role or function in international political practice.[11] Human rights are a class of norms that express minimum standards of treatment for individuals to which political communities can be held, and whose breach is a matter of international concern and may legitimize sovereignty-limiting measures, such as interventions in case of systematic human rights violations.[12] For present purposes, political conceptions in

---

particularly Western philosophical tradition and are thus not shared across cultures); Rorty (1993), p. 119 ('Since no useful work seems to be done by insisting on a purportedly ahistorical human nature, there probably is no such nature, or at least nothing in that nature that is relevant to our moral choices'); Ignatieff (2001), p. 55 (a historical justification of human rights 'need not make appeal to any particular idea of human nature').

[4] Winston (2007), p. 280; see also Cohen (2004), p. 192 (arguing for a justificatory minimalism that remains disconnected from 'a particular ethical or religious outlook'); for example, the Universal Declaration of Human Rights preamble, though casting human rights as 'inherent' (in the naturalistic sense), also alludes to far more pragmatic reasons for believing in human rights with historical reference to 'barbarous acts which have outraged the conscience of mankind'. See also Schulz and Raman (2020), p. 33.

[5] Winston (2007), p. 281f; see also Peters (2021a), p. 19 (arguing 'in favour of rights from a practical perspective, without speculating too much about the justification, simply pointing to the benefits of rights').

[6] Bobbio (1996), p. 18; see also Hunt (2007), p. 21 (noting that 'Human rights only become meaningful when they gain political content. They are not the rights of humans in a state of nature; they are the rights of humans in society').

[7] See e.g. Beitz (2009), p. xii ('"human rights" names not so much an abstract normative idea as an emergent political practice'); Hoffmann (2006), p. 405 (noting that from a non-foundationalist perspective, human rights 'are bound to mutate from an expression of the ontological essence of all human beings to a highly particular historical construct').

[8] Rawls (1999); Rawls (1993).

[9] Beitz (2009); Beitz (2004), p. 197 (noting that the 'functional role of human rights in international discourse and practice is regarded as definitive of the idea of a human right').

[10] Raz (2010).

[11] See Liao and Etinson (2012), p. 329.

[12] See Rawls (1999), p. 79 ('Human rights are a class of rights that play a special role in a reasonable Law of Peoples: they restrict the justifying reasons for war and its conduct, and they specify limits to a regime's internal autonomy'); Raz (2010), p. 328f ('human rights are those regarding which sovereignty-limiting measures are morally justified'); Beitz (2009), p. 31ff ('human rights are standards for the governments of states whose breach is a matter of international concern').

3.1 Human Rights Denaturalized: Constructing Rights on Practical Grounds

this narrow sense will not be explored further, as they do not seem immediately relevant to the animal question. While there is some evidence to suggest that the protection of animals is emerging as an international concern[13] and that animal interests may sometimes function as 'triggers for international intervention',[14] there is at present no sufficient state practice to validate the notion of animal rights as limits to state sovereignty.[15]

In a broader sense, political or practical conceptions of human rights encompass a range of historical, functionalist, constructivist, or experiential approaches and perspectives. Human rights are understood as a historically contingent and socially constructed normative paradigm that serves some important practical function, informed by past or present political needs and misdeeds.[16] According to the dominant narrative, human rights have emerged, consolidated, and expanded as political reactions to concrete experiences of suffering, violence, injustice, discrimination, oppression, slavery, genocides, and the horrors of two World Wars.[17] As Alan Dershowitz succinctly puts it, '*rights* come from *wrongs*'. On his 'experiential approach', rights are an 'experiential reaction to wrongs' and constructed from historical experiences of injustice.[18] Morton Winston describes human rights as 'normative responses to experiences of oppression' that are 'designed to prevent and ameliorate systematic or institutionalized forms of oppression.'[19] Conor Gearty submits that human rights serve the 'meta-idea' of protecting the politically weak

---

[13] See e.g. Sykes (2011); D'Amato and Chopra (1991), p. 50 (noting that 'International law can no longer be viewed as an artifact exclusively concerned with state and human interactions ... Rather, other living creatures in the environment are players in a new and expanded international legal arena').

[14] Cochrane (2013), p. 664 (arguing that 'states can and do intervene in the affairs of others for the sake of the basic interests of non-human sentient creatures').

[15] In a similar vein, Niesen (2020), p. 15f (noting that unlike human rights practice, there is not much animal rights practice from which to reconstruct a political conception of animal rights); but see Cruft et al. (2015), p. 20 (noting that it could be argued that the existence of a human right should not depend on whether there is an actual case for international concern, but on a principled assessment whether it should be of international concern. That is, human rights should 'guide actual practice rather than being determined by it').

[16] See e.g. Winston (2007), p. 284 (human rights as a 'socially constructed, historically evolved normative theory'); Schulz and Raman (2020), p. 33 (constructivist approaches as 'alternative for how we justify human rights claims ... human beings literally construct the rights they have').

[17] See e.g. Kreide (2015), p. 405 (noting that human rights grow from 'concrete experiences of injustice' and are 'political reactions to very specific threats, vulnerabilities, and forms of oppression'); Bobbio (1996), p. 18 (noting that 'human rights are historical rights which emerge gradually from the battles which human beings fight for their own emancipation').

[18] Dershowitz (2004), pp. 5–9 (further noting that 'As human beings have recognized the wrongs of such institutions as slavery, genocide ... they have constructed new rights to prevent the recurrence of old wrongs. It is no accident that the most important rights have often burgeoned in the immediate aftermath of the most horrendous wrongs').

[19] Winston (2007), p. 279, 284 (further noting that the essential purpose and function of human rights is 'to prevent and to eliminate those practices and social conditions that lead to, foster, support or directly cause severe, systematic oppression, or, put positively, to promote social conditions that

and vulnerable, and function as an 'emancipatory force against the abuse of power'.[20] Even more pragmatically, Michael Ignatieff asserts that while people may disagree about *why* we have human rights, they can agree *that* we need them: 'All that can be said about human rights is that they are necessary to protect individuals from violence and abuse, and if it is asked why, the only possible answer is historical.'[21] Human rights so denaturalized and politicized are thus stripped of their 'layers of philosophical and legal mystification',[22] and understood not as some innate quality that humans are magically born with, but as institutional responses to very real problems.

In this broader sense, political conceptions provide fertile grounds for fathoming the functionality of animal rights as new human rights. Political justifications of animal rights must advance practical or functional reasons why animals ought to have human rights. The following sections will explore two sets of practical reasons for animal rights: principled and prudential ones. The principled argument is that animals should have human rights for intrinsic reasons, to better protect them from violence, oppression, and exploitation. The prudential argument is that animal rights also serve the indirect function of better protecting the rights of humans, and are thus desirable even for purely instrumental, human rights-internal reasons.

3.2 The Principled Argument: Human Rights Are Good for Animals...

The principled argument for animal rights is primarily an ethical one. The core of it is that morality or justice[23] demands fundamental rights for animals, in order to address and alleviate the suffering, violence, oppression, extermination, and other injustices that animals experience in human societies. Over the past decades, variations of the justice-based case for animal rights have been formulated in moral, political, and

---

allow for human beings to live with their dignity, well-being, freedom, and their possibility of human flourishing intact.' Ibid., p. 286).

[20] Gearty (2009), pp. 178–80 (further noting that on a historical analysis, '"human rights" stops being a description of some essential truth about a species and becomes a subset of a larger idea – resistance to abusive power.' Ibid., p. 176).

[21] Ignatieff (2001), p. 55, 83; for a critical view on Ignatieff's minimalism and pragmatism, see Brown (2004).

[22] Gearty (2010), p. 11.

[23] See e.g. Nussbaum (2005), p. 319 ('a truly global justice requires not simply that we look across the world for other fellow species members who are entitled to a decent life. It also requires looking around the world at the other sentient beings').

legal philosophy.[24] Here, I will not delve into the moral reasoning whether and why animals *deserve* human rights, but instead focus on some of the practical reasons why animals might *need* them.[25] I will first outline the experiential backdrop that renders animals in need of the emancipatory resource of human rights, and then look at the (immediate) discursive, (eventual) institutional, and (long-term) transformative functions that human rights may serve for animals.

3.2.1 Human Rights as (Shared) Normative Resource against (Shared) Experiences of Injustice

Old human rights have emerged, and new human rights continue to emerge, as normative responses to entrenched or newly recognized forms of injustice. Our treatment and mass victimization of animals is increasingly perceived as 'one of the worst crimes in history'[26] and 'one of the great injustices of our time'.[27] Indeed, the human-animal relationship features some of the very themes of suffering, oppression, domination, and extermination that have operated as catalysts for the formation of human rights. Notably, animals experience widespread *suffering* and *death*,[28] institutionalized *violence*,[29] *discrimination*,[30] 'ubiquitous *domination* and

---

[24] See, notably, Nussbaum (2022); Korsgaard (2018); Cochrane (2018); Donaldson and Kymlicka (2011); Regan (2004); Cavalieri (2001); Rowlands (2002); Francione (2000); Wise (2000).

[25] I will also not deal with the general issue why animals need (subjective) rights instead of (objective) protection laws. That basic rights provide a stronger form of legal protection than mere human duties or animal protection laws has been argued elsewhere. For a general overview of the functional benefits of (fundamental) animal rights over animal welfare laws, see Stucki (2020), p. 552ff; Stucki (2016), p. 294ff; Peters (2021b), p. 482ff.

[26] Harari (2015).

[27] Wills (2018); Kymlicka and Donaldson (2016), p. 692 (noting that our 'treatment of animals is increasingly recognized as one of the greatest moral challenges we face … Just as current generations puzzle over our ancestors' endorsement of slavery, so future generations will wonder at our moral blindness about harms to animals'); Cao (2014), p. 169 ('our treatment of non-human animals is a major unresolved problem of social justice in the world today').

[28] For an overview of human practices causing widespread animal suffering and death, see e.g. Norwood and Lusk (2011); Clough (2018); Safran Foer (2009); Maher et al. (2017); Beirne (2009).

[29] See e.g. DeMello (2012), p. 236ff (noting that 'Institutionalized violence toward animals refers to the "regular" forms of violence toward animals that are part and parcel' of the economic and cultural fabric of our society); Cudworth (2015).

[30] Speciesism is commonly understood as a form of discrimination based on species-membership (akin to other forms of discrimination such as racism and sexism). See Horta and Albersmeier (2020).

oppression,³¹ and *zoocide* (a 'genocide' on species)³² at the hands of humans. Moreover, some argue that our systematic *exploitation*³³ of animals is akin to *slavery*;³⁴ that the systematic violence deployed against animals constitutes (literally or metaphorically) a *war* against animals;³⁵ and that the treatment of animals in factory farms may be comparable to *concentration camps*.³⁶ In short, the human-animal relationship is rife with atrocities that parallel many of the phenomena of injustice that have provided the experiential backdrop of human rights.³⁷

Given that the animal experience in many respects maps onto the human rights-generative experiential basis, it stands to reason that these shared experiences of injustice may warrant a shared normative response in the form of human rights. Human and animal rights are both informed by a background of historical and enduring experiences of suffering and injustice, and are driven by the political goal of ending the respective forms of oppression and social injustice.³⁸ Human rights have come to be 'the principle of liberation from oppression and domination',³⁹ and could very well grow into a political resource to address not only human

---

³¹ Jones (2015), p. 467 (emphasis added); see further Dubeau (2020); Gruen (1996, 2009); Nibert (2002, 2013); Scully (2003).

³² The unprecedented extinction of animal species due to human activities has been described as the 'sixth mass extinction' (or Anthropocene extinction). See Barnosky et al. (2011); Ceballos et al. (2015).

³³ On animal exploitation, see Zuolo (2020), p. 326 (defining exploitation as situations in which 'animals are instrumentally employed for the sake of producing something without taking their interests into account'); Korsgaard (2009), p. 14 (noting that we treat animals 'as mere means or obstacles to human ends' and discard of them when they have 'outlived their usefulness'); Stache (2020), p. 418 ('As super-exploited beings, animals do labour and produce products for free to the benefit of capital'); Gruen (2009), p. 162.

³⁴ See e.g. Pleasants (2008); Francione (2020), p. 30; Spiegel (1996); Donaldson and Kymlicka (2007), p. 189; Cavalieri (2001), p. 142.

³⁵ See Wadiwel (2015) (arguing that we should treat 'our systems of violence towards animals precisely as constituting a war'); Stucki (2023) (arguing that the normative regimes governing war and animal exploitation are comparable, and that animal welfare law functions like a warfare law).

³⁶ See notably Sztybel (2006) (himself the child of a Holocaust survivor, Sztybel argues that 'Although nothing occurring in the realm of oppression is ever quite the same as anything else ... in certain relevant respects, both broad and detailed comparisons can be made between the Holocaust and ... the oppression of animals. The real issue is not whether the comparison can be made ... the real question is whether we should dare to make the comparison, or to voice our opinions that there are chilling similarities between how Jews were treated in the Holocaust and how animals are treated in the present day'); see further Patterson (2002).

³⁷ Some people may object to comparisons between the suffering and oppression of humans and animals. However, as Kymlicka and Donaldson (2014), p. 119, submit, linking 'human and animal oppression is insulting to humans only if one starts from a commitment to species narcissism'; see also Spiegel (1996), p. 30.

³⁸ Much like human rights, one of the key political functions of animal rights lies in eliminating institutionalized oppression, 'abolishing exploitation and liberating animals from enslavement.' Donaldson and Kymlicka (2011), p. 49.

³⁹ Douzinas (2000), p. 1.

but also animal injustice.[40] It must be conceded, though, that unlike (most) humans, animals are unable to fight their own emancipatory battles. While animals may certainly commit individual acts of physical resistance against human aggressors,[41] they are not equipped to collectively act and organize resistance in the political arena.[42] Animals must therefore rely on human advocates to vindicate their best interests and rights vis-à-vis the political community. This element of paternalism—or solidarity[43]—is however not extraneous to the logic of human rights, whose 'power-taming'[44] function it is precisely to protect not just the power- and resourceful, but (perhaps even more so) the disempowered, vulnerable, and disenfranchised members of society.[45] This is not only true for children and humans with mental disabilities, who depend on individual guardians and political representatives to defend their human rights. It is more generally in the nature of systematic oppression that its (human) victims are 'essentially unable to rescue themselves' and experience a 'relative powerlessness ... to alter their situation through self-help alone'.[46] Anti-oppressive human rights are thus, to a greater or lesser extent, predicated on political solidarity and assistance by the non-oppressed and enfranchised. In this sense, human rights for animals need not necessarily be about *self*-emancipation, but rather, can function as a political 'vehicle for emancipation'.[47]

The overarching political goal of animal rights is to overcome the present societal conditions of institutionalized and oppressive violence against animals, and to advance the meta-idea of justice for animals. To this end, framing animal rights as new human rights can serve different practical functions of a short-term (discursive), medium-term (institutional), and long-term (transformative) nature.

---

[40] See e.g. Gearty (2009), p. 178 (noting that there is 'no inhibiting species barrier in play'); Nussbaum (2005), p. 300 (noting that 'There is no obvious reason why notions of basic justice, entitlement, and law cannot be extended across the species barrier'); Dershowitz (2004), p. 193, 199 (noting that animal rights 'may become established as the result of changing experiences'. Yet, he 'postpones the ultimate decision about broad-based animal rights to a future time when our history and experience no longer make them necessary for human use as food, clothing, or experimental subjects').

[41] On animal resistance, see Colling (2020); Hribal (2010).

[42] See also Pocar (1992), p. 221.

[43] Winston (2007), p. 287 (noting that the 'human rights ethos is founded on the notion of solidarity').

[44] Valentini (2017), p. 863 (characterizing the political function of human rights as 'placing constraints on the conduct of powerful actors').

[45] cf. Peters (2021a), p. 22 (noting that rights are 'needed exactly by the others, the ones who are deprived, and not by those who have the say and who have everything').

[46] Winston (2007), p. 287.

[47] Peters (2021a), p. 20; it may further be noted that the human-animal relationship is unequivocally of a social and political nature. Animals, whose lives and deaths are largely determined by human rules, are thus already subject to political power. See Niesen (2020), p. 10.

3.2.2 Discursive and Rhetorical Function

As was noted before, the gestation process of new human rights is a lengthy one.[48] Animal rights have passed the stage of intellectual conception and are currently in the emergence phase, awaiting broader institutional recognition. In this pre-institutional phase, the rhetoric of human rights plays an important role in social, political, and legal fora.[49] Indeed, using the language of human rights for animals is not altogether different from other new human rights claims, which are generally triggered by an *inadequate status quo* and serve a number of *rhetorical functions* on the path to *eventual institutionalization*.

New human rights claims have an 'appellative' or spotlighting function that draws attention to a hitherto unrecognized injustice or some existing state of inadequate protection for an important social value or vulnerable group.[50] The current state of animal protection—this much is agreed upon by all animal rights advocates—is painfully inadequate.[51] The (perceived) failure of existing animal welfare laws acts as a key political motive for transforming animals' real experiences of injustice into normative claims to human rights. Given the 'colossal appeal' of human rights to confront 'intense oppression or great misery',[52] it seems only natural for animal advocates to look to human rights discourse. Florian Hoffmann characterizes human rights as 'a plural, polycentric, and ultimately indeterminate discourse amenable to use by everyone nearly everywhere. Wherever individuals and groups wish to challenge what they perceive as oppressive or hegemonic structures, they can avail themselves of that discourse'.[53] Human rights may thus be understood as a kind of open source instrument that can be used by social justice movements, such as the animal rights movement,[54] for the political purpose of challenging, addressing, and

---

[48] See *supra* Chap. 1.1.3.

[49] On the rhetorical (appellative, contesting, connecting, triggering, and jurisgenerative) functions of new human rights, see generally von Arnauld and Theilen (2020).

[50] von Arnauld and Theilen (2020), p. 39f; Susi (2020), p. 22 (calling this the 'inadequacy of protection thesis').

[51] See e.g. Kymlicka (2017), p. 126 (noting the 'painful inadequacies of existing regimes of animal law' and that 'the fundamental purpose of these laws is not to protect animals, but on the contrary to assert the right to use animals'); Stucki (2023); Sankoff (2013); Bryant (2010), p. 59ff; DeCoux (2009), p. 19ff; on the shortcomings of current animal protection laws, see generally Francione (1995).

[52] Sen (2004), p. 317.

[53] Hoffmann (2006), p. 409 (further stating that 'There is no single correct signification and thus use of human rights'); see also Gearty (2010), p. 11 (characterizing human rights as 'vibrant, fluctuating, intentionally indefinable' term with a 'long and noble tradition as a galvanizer of resistance to oppression'); Kreide (2015), p. 410f (noting that the political language of human rights 'can be "used" by any person to criticize existing ordering structures and can be activated for political purposes' addressing oppression).

[54] On animal rights as a social justice issue, see e.g. Jones (2015); Kymlicka and Donaldson (2014), p. 116; Benton (1993); Nocella et al. (2014).

ultimately ending the identified injustice. Such is the mobilizing, contesting, and recognitional (or 'connecting') function of new human rights claims: they provide social movements with a powerful language for the 'contestation of an unjust status quo', the organization of opposition, and mobilization of societal support.[55]

Overall, new human rights claims are thus powerful 'challenges to the status quo' and its institutional arrangements, and offer a rhetorically potent instrument in the service of bringing about political and legal change.[56] Yet, for human rights claims to change realities, authoritative actors and institutions must recognize them.[57] Perhaps most importantly, then, the language of human rights serves a jurisgenerative function[58] and generates pressure for eventual institutionalization. As Regina Kreide notes, human rights claims do not only 'trigger processes of reflection about injustices but also give rise to expectations and "performance pressure" on the part of states', for example, to translate moral rights to legal rights.[59] Such is generally the function of moral rights claims as 'demand for new legal rights'[60]—what has been variously described as 'ought to be legal rights',[61] 'manifesto' rights or 'ideal rights'.[62] In this way, new human rights claims can serve as a 'bridge between morality and law'.[63]

---

[55] von Arnauld and Theilen (2020), p. 49; see also Gearty (2010), p. 11 et passim (viewing human rights 'as a phrase around which positions of opposition to power can be articulated, new bonds of solidarity can be garnered and fresh versions of right and justice can be launched on a disbelieving world'); Koskenniemi (2010), p. 48 ('To dress a claim ... in the form of a "right" is to put it in the strongest available terms').

[56] See Susi (2020), p. 22f.

[57] See Bob (2009), p. 10.

[58] Facilitating eventual jurisgenesis, i.e., the creation or reinterpretation of recognitional legal norms. See von Arnauld and Theilen (2020), p. 47f.

[59] Kreide (2015), p. 405.

[60] Feinberg (1992), p. 153 (moral rights assertion so as to 'put in a claim ... to be given the corresponding legal right').

[61] Stucki (2020), p. 534.

[62] Feinberg (1973), p. 67, 84f ('Ideal right' in the sense of 'what *ought* to be a positive ... right, and would be so in a better or ideal legal system').

[63] Bilchitz (2018), p. 128 (arguing that 'fundamental rights are best understood as moral ideals that create pressure for legal institutionalization'. Ibid, p. 121); see further Langlois (2016), p. 17 (noting that the 'historical development of human rights has depended on the conviction that rights exist as *moral demands* that need to be translated into legal and institutional contexts in order to be effectively protected').

3.2.3 Institutional and Universalizing Function

Institutionalization marks the transition from merely moral rights (claims) to legally recognized rights. Human rights are generally considered to be of a dual, moral and legal nature, and best understood as a 'legally recognized and enforceable subset of universal moral rights.'[64] As moral rights, human rights exist regardless of whether they are recognized, codified, respected, or enforced by law.[65] But human rights are also of an 'inherently legal nature'[66] and positivized in a canon of international and constitutional human rights law.[67] This process of positivization, juridification, or legalization[68] is important also for animal rights, because translating suprapositive rights into institutional contexts contributes to making the protection of animals more robust and effective.[69] Merely moral animal rights are not able to set the kind of 'real and substantial obstacles'[70] against institutionalized forms of injustice that human rights are expected to set. As Martha Nussbaum has aptly noted, 'No major crimes against sentient beings have been curbed by ethics alone, without the coercive force of law'.[71] Indeed, institutionalization constitutes the very essence of political conceptions of human rights, as 'rights which are to be given institutional recognition, rights which transcend private morality.'[72]

The legal institution of human rights protects fundamental interests that are 'typically threatened by the state',[73] and its main addressees are thus public institutions.[74] At present, states are heavily implicated in systematic (moral) animal rights violations, either by inflicting or facilitating collectively organized violence against animals.[75] The act of institutionalization would place states under a duty to respect, protect, and fulfil (legal) animal rights.[76] With regard to the *duty to respect*, an

---

[64] Besson (2015), p. 281.

[65] See Skorupski (2010), p. 358.

[66] Besson (2018), p. 28.

[67] See Winston (2007), p. 282; on the 'dual positivization' of fundamental rights (as international human rights and constitutional rights), see generally Neuman (2003), p. 1864ff.

[68] That is, 'the legal recognition and modulation of universal moral rights' as legal human rights. See Besson (2012), p. 240.

[69] See generally Neuman (2003), p. 1869.

[70] MacCormick (2008), p. 197 (noting that human rights 'set real and substantial obstacles to notorious and historically well attested ways of inflicting misery and degradation on humans').

[71] Nussbaum (2018), p. 2.

[72] Raz (2010), p. 335.

[73] Peters (2016), p. 43.

[74] See Besson (2015), p. 283.

[75] Lorite Escorihuela (2011), p. 26 (noting that 'States are simply engaged, as political organisations, and through the exercise of sovereign power, in massive violence against animals. At the peak of their agency, States support, sponsor, or even organize actual physical coercion against them').

[76] On the tripartite structure of human rights obligations, see generally Shue (1996), p. 53.

important function of legal animal rights would be to raise the burden of justification for infringements.[77] Whereas today, animals' fundamental interests are regularly overridden by inferior or even trivial human interests, interfering with fundamental animal rights would trigger more stringent justification requirements based on established principles of human rights adjudication. This would, first, limit the sorts of considerations that constitute a legitimate aim which can be balanced against fundamental animal rights. Furthermore, the balancing process must encompass a strict proportionality analysis, comprised of the elements of suitability, necessity and proportionality *stricto sensu*, which would preclude the bulk of the sorts of low-level justifications that are currently sufficient.[78] This heightened threshold for justifiable infringements, in turn, translates to a lower infringeability of fundamental animal rights and an increased immunisation of animals' *prima facie* protected interests against being overridden by conflicting considerations and interests of lesser importance.

While public actors frequently engage in animal rights violations, Anne Peters rightly notes that 'the most important direct abusers of animals are private actors . . . However, behind those private actors stands the regulation (or the regulatory failure) of states.'[79] Importantly, then, legal animal rights would impose on the state a *duty to protect*—a systemic responsibility to create and implement a legal system that protects animal rights also against private transgressions, through proper legislation and enforcement.[80] As Peters puts it, 'animal rights should be modelled on fundamental human rights, directed against the state, but unfolding appropriate "horizontal" effects against private actors.'[81] In this vein, the Constitutional Court of Ecuador held that the animal right to life comprises two dimensions: a negative one, through which the state is prohibited from infringing on animal life, and a positive one, through which public authorities are obliged to establish a system of rules that protect animal life against aggression regardless of their public or private origin.[82]

The Ecuadorian Constitutional Court further alluded to the state's *duty to fulfil*, when noting that the right to free development of animal behaviour includes not just the negative duty of the state or any other person not to interfere, impede, or hinder free development, but also the positive obligation of the state to promote and ensure the development of free animal behaviour.[83] The duty to fulfil generally describes

---

[77] See Stucki (2020), p. 555f.

[78] At present, the overwhelming portion of permissible interferences with animals' interests can hardly be said to be necessary or proportionate in any real sense of the word. See Francione (2000), p. 9, 55.

[79] Peters (2021b), p. 512.

[80] See generally Besson (2015), p. 283; Nickel (2007), p. 9f.

[81] Peters (2021b), p. 513.

[82] Corte Constitucional del Ecuador, Final Judgment No. 253-20-JH/22 ('Estrellita Monkey' case) of 27 January 2022, para 131f.

[83] Ibid, para 114.

the positive obligations of states to assist and provide the right-holders with access to the objects of their rights.[84] This means that formal legal recognition should successively lead to the substantive realization of animal rights.

Lastly, recognizing and institutionalizing animal rights as new human rights would also imply their (eventual) universalization.[85] Indeed, Anne Peters points out that animal rights 'need to be universalized in order to have an effect in a globalized setting.'[86] Against the backdrop of the 'globalization of animal cruelty'[87] and the transnational nature of animal exploitation,[88] human rights universalism offers a suitable conceptual framework for unfolding the basic, non-relational rights of all animals on a global scale, irrespective of an animal's particular circumstances, geographical background, or species. International animal rights could serve as a benchmark against which to measure, criticize, and develop domestic law that fails to satisfy international standards.[89] And while universalized animal rights, like human rights universalism, may attract the criticism of cultural imperialism, Costas Douzinas reminds us that 'Too often respect for cultural differences, a necessary corrective for the arrogance of universalism, has turned into a shield protecting appalling local practices.'[90]

3.2.4 Aspirational and Transformative Function

Formal legal recognition marks but a starting point—rather than the endpoint—for the realization of human and animal rights.[91] Once institutionalization has occurred, the long-term work in progress is to translate the moral ideals expressed in legal rights to real change. Respecting, protecting, and fulfilling animals' most fundamental rights would inevitably require far-ranging changes in our treatment of animals, and would ultimately rule out 'virtually all existing practices of the animal-use

---

[84] See generally Karp (2020), p. 86.

[85] As the Supreme Court of India has put it, the 'United Nations, all these years, safeguarded only the rights of human beings, not the rights of other species … International community should hang their head in shame, for not recognizing their rights'. Supreme Court of India 7 May 2014, civil appeal no 5387 of 2014, para 47.

[86] Peters (2018), p. 355.

[87] White and Cao (2016), p. 2.

[88] See Lorite Escorihuela (2011), p. 26 (noting the 'normalized global commodification of animals as goods, parts, products, and resources, exchanged across borders').

[89] See Peters (2018), p. 356.

[90] Douzinas (2000), p. 137; for an overview of the critique of legal imperialism and responses, see Peters (2021b), p. 558; see also Casal (2003).

[91] See Harvey (2004), p. 723 (noting that human rights are 'a work in progress rather than a finished project'); Kymlicka and Donaldson (2018), p. 333 (noting that 'achieving legal rights on paper is just one stage, not the end, of the political struggle').

industries'.[92] Considering how deeply animal exploitation is woven into the economic and cultural fabric of contemporary societies, and how pervasive violence against animals is on both an individual and a collective level, the idea of recognizing—let alone enforcing—animal rights may therefore appear far removed from social reality.[93] This chasm between normative ideals and the deeply imperfect realities they collide with—or what Jack Donnelly calls the 'possession paradox' ('"having" and "not having" a right at the same time')[94]—is however not a problem unique to fundamental *animal* rights. Rather, the idea of human rights is generally of an evolutionary and aspirational nature.[95] As Philip Harvey submits, virtually all human rights claims, when first formally recognized, were mere aspirations with little correspondence to reality. Moreover, human rights must always remain aspirational to some degree, in that they constantly expand and raise the bar for the to-be-achieved (yet presently unattainable) goals.[96] Human rights are thus 'a form of aspirational law' through which humans set goals for themselves concerning 'the kinds of societies they are committed to creating'.[97] Or as Patricia Williams puts it, 'rights are to law what conscious commitments are to the psyche'.[98] Aspirational rights express commitments to ideals that, even if they may not be fully realisable at the time of their formal recognition, act as a continuous reminder and impulse that stimulates social and legal change towards more expansive implementation.

This provides a useful lens for thinking about the aspirational nature and transformative function of fundamental animal rights. Surely, the mere formal recognition of fundamental animal rights will not, by any realistic measure, bring about an instant practical achievement of the ultimate goal of 'abolishing exploitation and liberating animals from enslavement'.[99] Take, for example, the right to life.

---

[92] Donaldson and Kymlicka (2011), p. 40; Regan (2004), p. 348f (noting that the ultimate conclusion of animal rights is 'the total dissolution of the animal industry as we know it').

[93] See also Bilchitz (2009), p. 69.

[94] Donnelly (2013), p. 9 (noting that paradoxically, '"having" a right is of most value precisely when one does not "have" (the object of) the right—that is, when active respect or objective enjoyment is not forthcoming').

[95] See generally Harvey (2004); Knowles (2001), p. 255f (noting that 'the human rights framework expresses both fundamental prescriptions on behavior and aspirational goals for society.... human rights instruments describe both minimum conditions for human flourishing and aspirational goals for a world in which all humans live in harmony and reach their fullest potential'); Nagan et al. (2016), p. 75 (noting that a 'political or legal idea is not necessarily one that is translated into operational practice. In modern terminology, it is a perspective.... History is a constant struggle to put man's ideas or perspectives into practice').

[96] Harvey (2004), p. 717f, 722 (noting that 'Rather than expressing the rules we currently are willing to live by, human rights norms tend always to exceed our reach. They are a kind of law by means of which human societies set goals for themselves').

[97] Harvey (2004), p. 723.

[98] Williams (1987), p. 424.

[99] Donaldson and Kymlicka (2011), p. 49.

Respecting and protecting animal life would (at least in industrialised societies) preclude most forms of killing animals for food, and would thus certainly conflict with the entrenched practice of eating meat. Yet, while the current social normality of eating animals may make an immediate prohibition of meat production and consumption unrealistic, this is also precisely the reason why animals need a right to life (i.e., a right not to be eaten), as fundamental rights help to denormalize accepted social practices and to establish, internalize, and habituate normative boundaries.[100] David Bilchitz proposes the established concept of 'progressive realisation' (originally developed in the context of socio-economic human rights) as a useful legal framework for the gradual implementation of animal rights. Accordingly, each fundamental animal right could be seen as comprising a *minimum core* that has to be ensured immediately, coupled with a general *prohibition of retrogressive measures* and an obligation to progressively move towards a *fuller realisation*.[101]

To be sure, achieving the full recognition and realization of animal rights will be a long, gradual, and perpetual process.[102] Although fundamental animal rights may currently not be fully realisable, the very act of introducing them into law and committing to them as normative ideals places animals on the political map and provides a powerful basis from which to address and alleviate the injustice suffered by animals in current societies. In this way, institutionalized animal rights can function as legal infrastructure for moving from an imperfect and unjust status quo towards more ideal societal conditions in which animal rights can be respected and protected.[103]

3.3   ... and Animal Rights Are Good for Humans: The Prudential Argument

The justice-based case for animal rights, on its own, will likely not convince the humanist sceptic. Granted, human rights may be good for animals—but are animal rights good for humans? While the principled argument for animal rights relies on practical reasons why animals stand to benefit from receiving human rights, the prudential argument must proffer compelling reasons why humans stand to benefit from giving human rights to animals. Prudential reasons for animal rights are such that can be arrived at from a purely *instrumental, human rights-internal* logic, insofar as animal rights simultaneously serve the indirect function of strengthening

---

[100] See Kymlicka and Donaldson (2018), p. 331f.

[101] Bilchitz (2010), p. 291ff.

[102] See also Bilchitz (2009), p. 69.

[103] Bilchitz (2018), p. 121ff, understands fundamental rights as 'bridging concepts' that facilitate the transition from past and present imperfect social realities towards more just societies.

human rights protection. Indeed, the prudential argument submits that human rights may function *better* in tandem with animal rights, and that ignoring animal rights will end up undermining human rights.

3.3.1 Antagonistic and Synergistic Assumptions

The general intuition, especially among human rights scholars, is that human rights best remain an exclusive 'humans only' club, if only for practical reasons, because recognizing animal rights would have negative effects on humans.[104] The common concern that animal rights are bad for human rights takes different forms. Some scholars generally caution against an excessive proliferation of rights, as it risks trivializing the institution and eroding the currency of human rights.[105] Others fear that admitting animals into the fundamental rights club would be a slippery slope, and level down the normative status of humans.[106] For example, Richard Posner advocates for keeping a strict dividing line between humans and animals, lest 'we may end up treating human beings as badly as we treat animals, rather than treating animals as well as we treat (or aspire to treat) human beings.'[107] In a similar vein, Richard Cupp projects that 'Rather than only seeing animals' rights status rise, we should expect also to see humans' rights status to fall, with human rights and animal rights meeting somewhere in the middle.'[108] Will Kymlicka and Sue Donaldson have further observed a 'distinctively Left motivation for resisting animal rights', namely the concern that they will harm 'the struggles of other disadvantaged groups.'[109] All of these objections rest on the (oftentimes implicit) assumption that the human rights project is predicated on a special, and elevated, human status—the hallmark of human exceptionalism. The bottom line of the antagonistic intuition is the expectation that animal rights would somehow undermine human rights, and that the ongoing exclusion of animals is therefore a necessary evil to the higher goal of safeguarding human rights.

Although these are important concerns that warrant serious consideration, I take the assumption of a principally antagonistic relationship between human and animal rights to be problematic and mistaken. The antagonistic assumption speculates about *potential negative* effects that may or may not actualize. Certainly, some old human rights would be incompatible with fundamental animal rights and would need to be

---

[104] See e.g. Schmahmann and Polacheck (1995), p. 749 (arguing that it would be 'dangerous to give or attribute legal rights to animals because such extension of legal rights would have serious, detrimental impacts on human rights and freedoms').

[105] See *supra* Chap. 1.2.

[106] On this concern, see Wills (2020) (arguing that such 'levelling-down' concerns are misplaced).

[107] Posner (2006), p. 61.

[108] Cupp (2009), p. 77f.

[109] Kymlicka and Donaldson (2014), p. 118.

retired, such as the right to injure and kill animals for culinary pleasure or entertainment. Suchlike entitlements to and powers over another's body might, however, be considered 'illegitimate rights' in the first place (as was historically the case with slave-owners' rights).[110] This is not to say that legitimate rights conflicts would not inevitably occur, for example, between equivalent human and animal interests to life, health, or habitat. To deal with these concrete rights conflicts, appropriate legal mechanisms will have to be developed, along the lines of the proportionality and balancing requirements guiding human rights adjudication.[111] But on a more abstract level, it is unclear why respect for animal rights would generally and necessarily be harmful to, and diminish respect for, human rights.[112] Animal rights advocates consistently emphasize that rather than devaluing humans, animal rights would simply upvalue animals and may even result in more respect for human rights.[113] For example, Anne Peters asserts that 'upgrading the cause of animals in no way inevitably downgrades concern for humans ... In theory, both agendas can go hand in hand. In practice, they normally do so.'[114]

Moreover, we may just as well assume that animal and human rights have an overall synergistic and mutually beneficial relationship, and consider the *potential positive* effects of this alliance.[115] Rather than undermining them, animal rights may actually bolster our commitment to human rights. In this vein, Helena Silverstein argues that affirming animal rights strengthens human rights in several ways: it reaffirms the rights of non-paradigmatic humans, reinforces the notion that 'arbitrary demarcations, including those that justify racism, sexism, and other "isms," are inappropriate', and champions the values of sentience and empathy.[116] We may call this the *synergistic approach*, one that 'reaffirms human rights and

---

[110] Wise (1998), p. 796 (noting that 'The unjustly enriched always suffer from the applications of justice' and that stripping away humans' property rights over animals 'threatens only illegitimate rights'); in a similar vein, but in the context of women's rights curtailing men's rights, MacKinnon (1993), p. 615 (noting that 'male forms of power over women are affirmatively embodied as individual rights in law. When men lose power, they feel they lose rights. Often they are not wrong.' What is eliminated, though, are 'current "rights" to use, access, possess, and traffic women').

[111] See Stucki (2020), p. 555f; Stucki (2023), chapter III.B.2; see also Fasel (2019), p. 168f.

[112] As Taylor (2010), p. 231, succinctly puts it: 'showing respect for animals (or women, or non-white people, or whomever) does not require or imply showing less respect for humans (or men, or white people, or whomever)'; see also Keim and Sosnowski (2012), p. 78 (arguing that the human and animal rights cause are not mutually exclusive).

[113] See e.g. Francione (2000), p. 174 (the 'argument for animal rights does not decrease respect for human life; it increases respect for all life').

[114] Peters (2016), p. 36.

[115] See also Kivinen (2021), p. 195ff (arguing that animal rights discourse should be more invested in furnishing arguments for animal rights that correspond with overlapping human interests); Regan (1985), p. 24 (stating that 'the animal rights movement is part of, not antagonistic to, the human rights movement').

[116] Silverstein (1996), p. 51.

concomitantly advances animal rights.'[117] The core of the synergistic argument is that because, and to the extent that, the social or natural conditions that threaten human and animal rights are intertwined, so should be the normative responses—interrelated problems call for interrelated solutions.[118] Put differently, in light of their social and natural interconnectedness, disrespecting animal rights is likely to harm human rights, and respect for animal rights is likely to benefit human rights.

While both the antagonistic and synergistic assumption ultimately remain speculative—one about potential harmful effects, the other about potential positive effects—there are a number of compelling reasons to think that human and animal rights are mutually reinforcing and beneficial in important respects. In the following, I will look at two prudential reasons in particular—one of a socio-political and one of an eco-political nature—that should incline us to adopt a synergistic understanding. The first reason why we should understand human and animal rights as interdependent is that the underlying rights-generative phenomena of social injustice are interconnected and can fully be addressed only jointly. The second reason is that institutionalized animal exploitation feeds into and exacerbates a range of (anthropogenic) environmental problems—such as climate change, biodiversity loss, and zoonotic diseases—that pose some of the gravest existential threats to human rights.

3.3.2 Interconnections Between (Human and Animal) Rights-Generative Phenomena of Social Injustice

One of the key practical goals of human rights is to eliminate or alleviate 'the major forms of institutionalized oppression'[119] and other forms of social injustice experienced by humans around the world. According to the synergistic argument, human rights may be better equipped to fulfil this function by integrating and simultaneously tending to animal rights. This is because many of the human rights-generative phenomena of social injustice appear to be interlinked with those underlying animal rights. That is, social injustice against animals in many ways interacts with, amplifies, and serves to justify injustices towards other humans, and thus works to undermine the emancipatory mandate of human rights.

---

[117] Silverstein (1996), p. 51.

[118] There is a multitude of ways in which human welfare and rights intersect with animal welfare and rights. See e.g. Peters (2021b), p. 41ff (noting that the exploitation of animals raises or exacerbates a range of problems for human societies, the environment, and the planet, such as resource-inefficiency, global warming, food insecurity and diet-related diseases, and even armed conflicts and piracy. She concludes that 'animal use contributes to problems of global nature and proportions: ecological damage, the extinction of species, human poverty and malnutrition, organised crime and war'); Matsuoka and Sorenson (2013) (arguing that human social welfare needs to include animal welfare, given the harmful consequences of animal exploitation on human health, vulnerable groups, and the environment).

[119] Winston (2007), p. 285.

3.3.2.1 Intersections Between Human and Animal Social Justice Movements

Since the late eighteenth century, we can find numerous instances of intellectual and practical interconnections between human and animal social justice movements, demonstrating a lived political alliance.[120] Historical links of animal rights exist, for example, with abolitionist, pacifist, humanitarian, and socialist values. As Conor Gearty notes, the 'move towards compassion for animals . . . was not very different in sentiment from the feelings which produced the anti-slavery and humanitarian movements of the same period.'[121]

For example, the philosopher and social reformer Jeremy Bentham (1748–1832) compared the injustice of animals' treatment with that of slaves:

> The day has been . . . in which the greater part of the species, under the denomination of slaves, have been treated by the law exactly upon the same footing as . . . the inferior races of animals are still. The day *may* come, when the rest of animal creation may acquire those rights which never could have been withholden from them but by the hand of human tyranny. The French have already discovered that the blackness of the skin is no reason why a human being should be abandoned without redress to the caprice of a tormentor. It may come one day to be recognized, that the number of the legs, the villosity of the skin, or the termination of the *os sacrum*, are reasons equally insufficient for abandoning a sensitive being to the same fate? . . . the question is not, Can they *reason*? nor, Can they *talk*? but, Can they *suffer*?[122]

The social reformer and humanitarian Henry Stephens Salt (1851–1939) was one of the founders of the Humanitarian League, a 'radical pressure group' that espoused both human and animal rights and campaigned against corporal and capital punishment, sports hunting, and vivisection.[123] Salt also authored one of the earliest and most comprehensive treatises on animal rights, which he related to human rights and social progress:

> If "rights" exist at all . . . they cannot be consistently awarded to men and denied to animals, since the same sense of justice and compassion apply in both cases . . . It is an entire mistake to suppose that the rights of animals are in any way antagonistic to the rights of men. Let us not be betrayed for a moment into the specious fallacy that we must study human rights first, and leave the animal question to solve itself hereafter; for it is only by a wide and disinterested study of *both* subjects that a solution of either is possible.[124]

---

[120] For a history of the animal rights movement and its intersections with human social justice movements, see generally Traïni (2016).

[121] Gearty (2009), p. 179 (further noting that 'The underlying idea behind each of these progressive movements was a strong commitment to the protection of the vulnerable (slaves/captured soldiers) from abuse of power (by their owners/captors). The analogy with the animal welfare movement, which was building a strong momentum at the same time, is clear.' Ibid., p. 180).

[122] Bentham (1789), p. 309.

[123] On the Humanitarian League, see Weinbren (1994).

[124] Salt (1894), p. 19, 21.

The philosopher and socialist Leonard Nelson (1882–1927)—who founded the Militant Socialist International (*Internationaler Sozialistischer Kampfbund*), which was part of the resistance against German National Socialism—also wrote about animal rights in his work.[125] He connected the emancipatory labour movement and class struggle with the exploitation of animals and vegetarianism:

> A labourer who does not just want to be a 'prevented capitalist' and who is thus serious about the fight against all exploitation, does not bow to the nefarious habit of exploiting harmless animals and does not take part in the everyday murder of millions of animals, whose cruelty, barbarity, and cowardice dwarfs the horrors of the world war.[126]

Perhaps the strongest historical link of animal rights is with the women's rights movement.[127] Numerous women's suffrage campaigners simultaneously advocated against animal cruelty. For example, Frances Power Cobbe (1822–1904)—a social reformer, suffragette, and founder of several animal advocacy groups (such as the National Anti-Vivisection Society)—was (in)famous both for her women's rights and animal rights activism. These nineteenth century connections between feminism and animal causes were 'precursors of a generation yet to come'—ecofeminists.[128] According to Greta Gaard, one of the mothers of ecofeminism,

> Ecofeminism is a theory that has evolved from various fields of feminist inquiry and activism: peace movements, labor movements, women's health care, and the anti-nuclear, environmental, and animal liberation movements. Drawing on the insights of ecology, feminism, and socialism, ecofeminism's basic premise is that the ideology which authorizes oppressions such as those based on race, class, gender, sexuality, physical abilities, and species is the same ideology which sanctions the oppression of nature. Ecofeminism calls for an end to all oppressions ... Its theoretical base is a sense of self ... that is interconnected with all life.[129]

Core to ecofeminism is an understanding of the interlocking oppression of animals, women (whose inferiority has historically been constructed by likening them to animals), and other marginalized humans.[130] This interconnectedness of human and animal oppression is also a key theme in Critical Animal Studies, whose intersectional social justice approach seeks to achieve both human and animal liberation.[131] In political practice, the interlinkage of social justice for humans and

---

[125] See e.g. Nelson (1949).

[126] Nelson (1972), p. 376 (translation mine): 'Ein Arbeiter, der nicht nur ein "verhinderter Kapitalist" sein will und dem es also Ernst ist mit dem Kampf gegen jede Ausbeutung, der beugt sich nicht der verächtlichen Gewohnheit, harmlose Tiere auszubeuten, der beteiligt sich nicht an dem täglichen millionenfachen Tiermord, der an Grausamkeit, Roheit und Feigheit alle Schrecknisse des Weltkrieges in den Schatten stellt.'

[127] See e.g. Gaarder (2011); Kemmerer (2011).

[128] See e.g. Birke (2000).

[129] Gaard (1993b), p. 1.

[130] Gruen (1996), p. 441 ('animals are oppressed in ways not unlike the ways that women, people of color, and other groups are oppressed'); Adams and Donovan (1995); Gaard (1993a); Donovan and Adams (1996); Adams and Gruen (2014); MacKinnon (2005).

[131] See e.g. Deckha (2012); Nocella et al. (2014); Nibert (2002).

animals finds its clearest expression in the 'One Struggle'[132] slogan frequently promulgated by the animal rights movement: '"one struggle" against all forms of domination', and 'one struggle against exploitation'.[133]

Although much of intellectual and practical human rights work since the Enlightenment has been marked by human exceptionalism and the devaluation and exclusion of animals, there are many counterexamples of lived political interconnections between human and animal rights. While these examples are merely anecdotal, the underlying sentiment—that human and animal social (in)justice are interrelated—is increasingly corroborated by scientific research on the socio-psychological nexus between prejudicial attitudes against (marginalized) humans and animals, individual violence against (vulnerable) humans and animals, and collective violence against (animalized) humans and animals.

3.3.2.2 Sexism, Racism, Speciesism: The Correlation Between Prejudicial Attitudes Against (Marginalized) Humans and Animals

Human rights seek to eliminate deeply rooted forms of discrimination against humans based on their sex, ethnicity, nationality, cultural or religious background, sexual orientation, etc. The prudential argument for animal rights draws on an observed correlation between discriminatory attitudes towards human outgroups and speciesist attitudes,[134] suggesting an 'important link between one's disposition toward human and nonhuman animals'.[135] Research from social psychology indicates that prejudicial attitudes (such as sexism and racism) towards marginalized humans are generally associated with, and fostered by, prejudicial attitudes towards animals (speciesism).[136] Studies have also shown that 'endorsing speciesist attitudes is significantly and positively associated with negative attitudes toward ethnic outgroups'[137] and sexism,[138] and that people who eat meat show a stronger predisposition to prejudicial tendencies, authoritarianism, and social dominance

---

[132] A common chant at animal rights demonstrations goes like this: 'Human freedom, animal rights – one struggle, one fight.'

[133] Jenkins and Stanescu (2014), p. 74f.

[134] See Wills (2020), p. 220; Kymlicka (2018), p. 781 (highlighting the 'cascading set of negative effects on the rights of humans' that go along with human supremacism: it 'exacerbates racism, sexism and other forms of dehumanization, deadens ethical sensibilities, and marginalizes vulnerable human groups').

[135] Nibert (1994), p. 115.

[136] See Costello and Hodson (2010, 2014); Plous (2003) (highlighting the socio-psychological parallels between prejudice against human outgroups and prejudice against animals).

[137] Dhont et al. (2014), p. 105, 107 (showing that 'biases toward human outgroups are intrinsically related to biases toward non-human animals because a general desire for group-based dominance and inequality underpin both types of biases').

[138] Roylance et al. (2016).

orientation (as compared to vegetarians and vegans).[139] That is, many of the psychological factors – such as power, dominance, and control—underlying the speciesist mindset also 'serve to reinforce and promote prejudice against humans.'[140] According to the *Interspecies Model of Prejudice*, this correlation can be explained by the exceptionalist belief in a human-animal divide, which sets the foundation for hierarchical thinking about animals *and* human outgroups (marginalized 'others' that are often likened *to* animals).[141]

The growing evidence on the socio-psychological interconnections between speciesist and intrahuman discriminatory attitudes seems to repudiate the antagonistic assumption that animal rights must be sacrificed for the benefit of human rights. Rather, the reverse appears more likely: that *disregard* for animal rights may have negative effects on humans, by reinforcing the very (intrahuman) prejudices that human rights are supposed to fight.[142] Considering that speciesism operates as a 'multiplier of oppressive theories, attitudes, beliefs and practices that negatively affect marginalized humans', Joe Wills rightly proposes that animal rights should be seen as 'part of the solution to discrimination against marginalized humans, not as part of the problem'.[143]

3.3.2.3 Dehumanization and Animalization: The Link Between (Collective) Violence Against Humans and Animals

Closely related to the aforementioned nexus between discriminatory *mindsets* towards humans and animals, there further exists a well-established link between *physical violence* against humans and animals.

On the level of individual or *interpersonal violence*, animal abuse has long been associated with violent crimes against humans and other antisocial behaviour.[144] Animal cruelty is often regarded as a 'gateway crime', and an indicator of someone's later propensity for (extreme) violence such as serial homicide, sexual assault, and school shootings.[145] Furthermore, regardless of whether animal abuse is believed to be predictive of interpersonal violence,[146] it is well-known to co-occur with

---

[139] Veser et al. (2015); Stone (2022).

[140] Plous (2003), p. 510.

[141] Costello and Hodson (2014), p. 177f; see also Kymlicka (2018), p. 773 (noting that 'Belief in human superiority over animals is not only empirically correlated with, but also causally connected to, the dehumanization of human outgroups').

[142] See Costello and Hodson (2010), p. 19 ('many of our outgroup biases may find their origins in our disregard for animal rights').

[143] Wills (2020), p. 199.

[144] See e.g. Arluke et al. (1999); Linzey (2009); Nurse (2016), p. 37ff; DeMello (2012), p. 245ff; Lucia and Killias (2011).

[145] See National Sheriffs' Association (2018), p. 5f; Beirne (2004); Bucchieri (2016).

[146] Sceptical notably Marceau (2019), p. 193ff (submitting that the predictive value of the 'link thesis' or 'progression thesis' is empirically flawed).

domestic violence against women and children, as an 'abusive household' tends to victimize all vulnerable family members.[147] It thus seems reasonable to assume that promoting respect for animal rights could simultaneously have 'the "tangible" benefit of preventing violence towards humans and anti-social behavior that has a negative impact on society'.[148]

Of even greater import to human rights is the link between *collective violence against humans and institutionalized (socially cultivated and condoned) violence against animals*.[149] Some of the gravest human rights violations have historically occurred and continue to happen during episodes of collective violence, such as wars and genocides. These acts of mass violence are regularly preluded by dehumanizing the victims and likening them to animals.[150] For example, during World War II, Jews in Nazi Germany were portrayed as vermin ('rats') and Japanese in America as 'monkeys' or 'apes', and during the Rwandan genocide, Tutsi were labelled 'cockroaches'. *Animalistic dehumanization*[151]—a type of dehumanization that operates through animalization—is a recurring epiphenomenon of and psychological justification for human mass violence.[152] Likening humans to animals marks them as less-than-human or subhuman, and works as a 'psychological lubricant' that lowers inhibitions against violence and enables the kind of destructiveness and cruelty that would be unthinkable in ordinary circumstances.[153]

Animalistic dehumanization feeds on, and derives its meaning from, the 'fundamental sacrifice of *nonhuman animals*' in our society.[154] That is, collective violence

---

[147] See e.g. Upadhya (2014); Faver and Strand (2003).

[148] Nurse (2016), p. 38.

[149] Beirne (2009), pp. 182–187 submits that when exploring the link between violence against humans and animals, we should expand our perspective from 'individual animal cruelty to institutionalized animal abuse.' He notes that the 'link between animal abuse and interhuman violence must surely be sought not only in the personal biographies of those individuals who abuse or neglect animals but also in those institutionalized social practices where animal abuse is routine, widespread, and often defined as socially acceptable'; see also Knight and Watson (2017).

[150] See e.g. Livingstone Smith (2011), p. 3, 13 (noting that 'dehumanization plays a crucial role in war, genocide, and other forms of brutality' and typically figures as a 'prelude and accompaniment to extreme violence').

[151] See Haslam (2006).

[152] See Haslam (2014), p. 43 (noting that 'the best known and least ambiguous historical examples of dehumanization involve animal metaphors').

[153] See Livingstone Smith (2011), p. 13; Fromm (1973), p. 123 ('Whenever another being is not experienced as human, the act of destructiveness and cruelty assumes a different quality'); Haslam et al. (2007), p. 409f (noting that 'inhumane actions are easier to perpetrate when their victims are seen as less than human' and that 'dehumanization enables, disinhibits, and justifies violent and otherwise aggressive behavior').

[154] Wolfe (2003), p. 101 (noting that animalization 'is linked to the ongoing practices of violence against non-human others ... [It] takes for granted the fundamental sacrifice of *nonhuman animals* ... which must continue to be legitimized if the ideological work of marking human others as animals for the purposes of their objectification and sacrifice is to be effective').

3.3 ... and Animal Rights Are Good for Humans: The Prudential Argument

against *metaphorically* animalized humans is informed and powered by a cultural backdrop of socially organized and normalized violence against *actual* animals.[155] Animalization works to disinhibit and justify violence against humans only because—encoded in and enforced through our everyday practices of institutionalized violence against real animals—the 'animal' signifies a position of inferiority, 'socially sanctioned abjection', and a legitimate target of instrumental violence.[156] The 'animal' designation offers a vast repertoire of socially habituated forms of cruelty that can be unleashed upon humans through the psychological mechanism of animalization. Consider the following passage in Theodor Adorno's *Minima Moralia*:

> The constantly encountered assertion that savages, blacks, Japanese are like animals, monkeys for example, is the key to the pogrom. The possibility of pogroms is decided in the moment when the gaze of a fatally-wounded animal falls on a human being. The defiance with which he repels this gaze – "after all, it's only an animal" – reappears irresistibly in cruelties done to human beings, the perpetrators having again and again to reassure themselves that it is "only an animal", because they could never fully believe this even of animals.[157]

This suggests that as long as our society practices itself in the normalization and rationalization of violence against sentient beings perceived as others, this pattern of desensitization, indifference, and cognitive dissonance exercised and cultivated on animals is always in standby mode, ready to be activated against human others.[158] The foreground actuality of institutionalized violence against animals thus operates as the permanent background potentiality of collective violence against animalized humans.

The nexus between mass violence against humans and animals through the interlocking mechanisms of dehumanization and animalization should incline human rights scholars (especially of the exceptionalist and antagonistic variant) to face an inconvenient truth: human exceptionalism is toxic not just for animals, but

---

[155] See e.g. Adams (2013), p. 69 (noting that the 'interaction between physical oppression and the dependence on [animal] metaphors ... indicates that we distance ourselves from whatever is different by equating it with something we have already objectified'); Lorite Escorihuela (2011), p. 27 (noting that 'Our millennial relationship to animals is ... the background to the possibility of treating humans as less, or other, than humans'); Hodson et al. (2014), p. 86 (noting that 'devaluing ... animals paves the way for the neglect, exploitation, or extermination of other humans metaphorically likened to such animals').

[156] See Boggs (2010), p. 99; Deckha (2012), p. 220.

[157] Adorno (2005), p. 105; in a similar vein, Kundera (1999), p. 286 ('Mankind's true moral test, its fundamental test ... consists of its attitude towards those who are at its mercy: animals. And in this respect mankind has suffered a fundamental débâcle, a débâcle so fundamental that all others stem from it').

[158] See e.g. Patterson (2002), p. 12 ('Once animal exploitation was institutionalized and accepted as part of the natural order of things, it opened the door to similar ways of treating other human beings, thus paving the way for such atrocities as human slavery and the Holocaust').

also for humans.[159] Animalistic dehumanization is inextricably intertwined with the ideology of human exceptionalism.[160] Indeed, animalization equals dehumanization only *within* the binary logic of human exceptionalism.[161] Recall that human exceptionalism rests on a conception of human nature that defines humanness in terms of *unique* features that separate (superior) humans from (inferior) animals. It is precisely this exceptionalist sense of unique humanness that is being denied to (dehumanized) humans when they are likened to animals.[162] The human rights-relevant problem with the human-animal divide is that the 'animal' category is malleable, rarely ever confined to actual animals, and can be 'ideologically deployed' against other humans.[163] Put differently, the human-animal binary is not merely a descriptive-zoological scheme that neatly separates all humans from all animals, but rather, a 'discursive resource'[164] that 'has historically produced and may continue to reproduce a bloody margin of subhumans'.[165]

Against the antagonistic assumption, it therefore seems to be the ideology of human exceptionalism (rather than animal rights) that undermines human rights. In fact, respect for animal rights would effectively disarm the psychological mechanism of animalization by erasing its violent meaning. As Scott Plous suggests, 'the very act of "treating people like animals" would lose its meaning if animals were treated well.'[166]

---

[159] See Hodson et al. (2014), p. 106 (noting that 'overvaluing humans, relative to nonhumans, lies at the heart of problems not only for animals but also for humans'); Costello and Hodson (2014), p. 177f (noting that exceptionalist 'ideology justifies the social legitimacy of dominating and exploiting non-human animals ... Troublingly, human domination over animals may also justify interhuman domination including slavery, genocide, and intergroup prejudices or violence').

[160] See Costello and Hodson (2014), p. 178 (noting that 'fundamental beliefs in a human-animal divide set the foundation for outgroup dehumanization').

[161] It is only within the ideological mindset of human exceptionalism, where being human precisely means *not* to be an animal, that 'animalization operates as an ongoing threat of dehumanization'. Deckha (2012), p. 219.

[162] Dehumanization in general is the negation of humanness, and animalistic dehumanization in particular is the negation of unique humanness in the exceptionalist sense that distinguishes humans from animals. See Haslam (2006), p. 257f; see also Hetey and Eberhardt (2014), p. 147 ('Thinking of humans as animals dehumanizes them by divesting them of uniquely human characteristics such as rationality, morality, and civility').

[163] Fox (2004), p. 477; Donaldson and Kymlicka (2007), pp. 192–194 (noting that 'Throughout history many members of the human species have been relegated to the "animal" side of the line'); Rorty (1993), p. 113 ('the line between humans and animals is not simply the line between featherless bipeds and all others ... the line divides some featherless bipeds from others').

[164] Wolfe (2013), p. 10 (noting that 'the distinction "human/animal"—as the history of slavery, colonialism, and imperialism well shows—is a discursive resource, not a zoological designation').

[165] Weitzenfeld and Joy (2014), p. 6.

[166] Plous (2003), p. 510.

3.3.2.4 'Entangled Empathy'[167] and 'Interspecies Solidarity'[168]

Winston Nagan and colleagues note that human rights violations are often driven by 'the emotion of negative sentiment which emerges as hate directed at the non-self "other"', and thus by cognitive processes 'devoid of affection, empathy or solidarity.' On the other side, they identify the generation of positive sentiment in the form of empathy, compassion, and solidarity as 'the driving force for a world culture of human rights'.[169] In a similar vein, Frederik von Harbou argues that human rights have their foundation in the natural faculty of empathy.[170] Perhaps most prominently, Richard Rorty offers a narrative of the human rights success story that rehabilitates 'the role of emotion and recognition of suffering',[171] and centres on sentimentality, sympathy, and solidarity (rather than rational morality).[172] Rorty pragmatically states that the 'emergence of the human rights culture seems to owe nothing to increased moral knowledge, and everything to hearing sad and sentimental stories'.[173] Human rights progress hinges on (privileged) people sympathizing with the suffering of the 'the despised and oppressed,'[174] and thus lives off empathy—the ability to relate to, and care about, someone else's suffering. For a sympathy-based human rights culture to flourish, we need what Rorty calls a 'sentimental education' that cultivates among people an 'increasing ability to see the similarities between ourselves and people very unlike us as outweighing the differences.'[175] It is this sense of commonality and kinship that helps different kinds of people to link up into 'a "planetary community" dominated by a culture of human rights'.[176] Rorty further alludes to the 'possibility of trans-species solidarity',[177] by suggesting that the sort of sentimentally educated, nice people who believe that 'prejudice against racial or religious groups is a terrible thing' might also be convinced 'to stop eating animals.'[178] This is because empathy redirects our focus onto the basic similarities that connect rather than the morally irrelevant differences

---

[167] Gruen (2015).

[168] Coulter (2016).

[169] Nagan et al. (2016), p. 1.

[170] von Harbou (2014).

[171] Abbey (2017), p. 13.

[172] In a similar vein, Hunt (2007), p. 26 (arguing that human rights depend 'on emotions as much as on reason').

[173] Rorty (1993), p. 118f.

[174] Rorty (1993), p. 127.

[175] Rorty (1993), p. 129.

[176] Rorty (1993), p. 125.

[177] Abbey (2017), p. 7.

[178] Rorty (1993), p. 126f; elsewhere, Rorty (1999), p. 79, notes that human rights culture depends on empathetic people 'to whom the hunger and suffering of *any* human being (and even, perhaps, that of any other animal) is intensely painful'; see also Abbey (2017), p. 8.

that separate us as humans—and these relevant similarities are such 'that do not interestingly distinguish us from many nonhuman animals.'[179]

Research from social psychology seems to corroborate the Rortyan supposition that the same kind of sentimentally educated people who have sympathy for *human others* are likely to have compassion for *other animals*—and vice versa. Previously, we noted the interlinkages between prejudicial attitudes and violence against humans and animals. The other, brighter side of this nexus is that positive and rights-affirming attitudes towards humans and animals appear to be equally interlinked. Yon Soo Park and Benjamin Valentino have found a 'strong connection between recognition of human rights and animal rights' both at the individual attitude and the policy level.[180] Their findings suggest that people's views about human and animal rights are tightly linked: 'People who believe in extending greater rights and protections to disadvantaged and marginalised groups ... also tend to be supportive of animal rights.'[181] Conversely, other studies have shown that emphasizing 'the basic capacities shared by humans and animals has the effect of expanding moral concern, not only to animals but also to human outgroups.'[182] In short, greater concern for animal rights seems to correlate with greater concern for human rights.[183]

Of course, the likely explanation for this is that empathy for humans and other sentient animals is naturally linked, because the sympathy-triggering suffering of human and nonhuman animals is in many respects similar.[184] Whereas it is sometimes assumed, in line with the antagonistic intuition, that humans should first care about other humans before caring about animals, Carol Adams asserts that such a 'hierarchy of caring' is mistaken. Rather, violence *against* and compassion *for* humans and animals are interdependent, and caring about both is required.[185] The sentimental education needed for a strong, sympathetic human rights culture ought thus to include a *humane* education that cultivates a sense of interspecies kinship and

---

[179] Rorty (1993), p. 129.

[180] Park and Valentino (2019), p. 39.

[181] Park and Valentino (2019), p. 63.

[182] Bastian et al. (2012), p. 427 (further explaining that 'Seeing animals as similar to humans triggers greater moral concern by highlighting their morally relevant capacities ... this process also naturally highlights that these same capacities are shared by all humans, thereby triggering increased moral concern for human outgroups').

[183] See also Wills (2020), p. 218; Stone (2022).

[184] See Stone (2022) (identifying 'empathy as an underlying common factor' that explains the correlation between positive attitudes towards human and animal rights); Beirne (2009), p. 187; Darwin (1871), p. 101 ('Sympathy beyond the confines of man, that is, humanity to the lower animals ... seems to arise incidentally from our sympathies becoming more tender and more widely diffused, until they are extended to all sentient beings').

[185] Adams (2007), p. 21f; the feminist care tradition proposes that 'sympathy, compassion, and caring are the ground' upon which animal rights should be constructed. See Donovan (2007), p. 174.

kindness—this promises to generate beneficial sentiments and outcomes for both humans and animals.[186]

3.3.2.5 Moving from a Culture of Cruelty to a Human Rights Culture of Compassion

Contrary to the antagonistic assumption, animal rights appear to be conducive to a more inclusive, respectful, and compassionate human rights culture based on (transspecies) sympathy and solidarity. In fact, the foregoing suggests that it is not animal rights, but rather, the ideology of human exceptionalism and disregard for animal rights that is positively harmful to human rights. If human rights culture is (at least partly) based on empathy and compassion, it seems easy to see how our culture of cruelty against animals ends up hurting human rights too. Cultivating violence against animals deadens our natural feelings of empathy and desensitizes us to the suffering not only of animal others, but also of other humans.[187] Conversely, cultivating refined compassion on both ends is good for human and animal rights. The very sentiments of empathy and kinship that underlie the recognition of animal rights will only work to foster and reinforce a compassionate human rights culture.[188] Indeed, practicing transspecies sympathy and solidarity may move us from a culture of cruelty to a true human rights culture of compassion.[189]

Overall, there are thus strong prudential reasons for recognizing animal rights as integral part of the human rights mandate.[190] Considering the socio-psychological interconnections between prejudice and violence against, and empathy and compassion for, humans and animals, protecting human and animal rights in concert seems to be the *functionally better normative response* to the human rights-relevant problems of oppression, discrimination, collective violence, and dehumanization.

---

[186] See Kymlicka (2018), p. 774 (noting that 'humane education regarding animals—emphasizing interspecies affinities and solidarities—is known to encourage greater empathy and pro-social attitudes towards other humans'); Costello and Hodson (2014), p. 193 (highlighting the promise of dismantling the human-animal divide 'as a possible prejudice intervention').

[187] Even though our culture of cruelty works to deaden our feelings of empathy for the masses of animals we exploit, most people cringe when confronted with *sad and sentimental stories* about individual animals and the horrors that are forced upon them. As Donaldson and Kymlicka (2007), p. 204, submit, perhaps these sentiments reflect our 'true moral intuition.'

[188] The more empathetic people we raise, 'the stronger and more global our human rights culture will become.' Rorty (1993), p. 127.

[189] As Marcuse (1965), p. 82, noted many decades ago, the 'elimination of violence, and the reduction of suppression to the extent required for protecting man and animals from cruelty and aggression are preconditions for the creation of a humane society'.

[190] See also Peters (2018), p. 360 (noting that an 'international animal rights codification would not only mitigate animal suffering but also would create positive synergies with the UDHR towards fulfilling its core mission, which is to prevent the commission of "barbarous acts which [outrage] the conscience of mankind"').

3.3.3 The Environmental Nexus Between Human and Animal Rights

The second prudential reason for animal rights is of an eco-political nature and derives not from the socio-political but from the environmental interconnectedness of human and animal rights. In the present era of the Anthropocene, some of the most pressing and existential threats to human rights—such as climate change and pandemics—are closely linked to our systematic exploitation and extermination of animals. The current state of 'planetary emergency'[191] provides perhaps the strongest incentive for integrating concern for animal rights into the human rights mandate. The prudential argument here is fairly straightforward and its scientific basis well-established. Therefore, the following will be limited to a brief outline of the human rights-relevant environmental problems and their nexus to animals, before extrapolating the indirect function that animal rights might serve with a view to better protecting human rights in the Anthropocene.

3.3.3.1 Environmental Threats to Human Rights and Their Links to Animal Exploitation

As was noted earlier, human rights growth is stimulated by changing material conditions, and new human rights emerge in response to novel threats to humanity.[192] Today, some of the most momentous natural (albeit anthropogenic) risks to human rights stem from climate change and other environmental degradation. The UN Special Rapporteur on Human Rights and the Environment, David Boyd, states that we are 'in the midst of an unprecedented environmental crisis'.[193] The world is facing climate emergency;[194] rising sea levels and temperatures;[195] potentially catastrophic biodiversity loss[196] (the 'sixth mass extinction'[197]); other environmental degradation such as deforestation, air, land, and water pollution; and

---

[191] Lenton et al. (2019), p. 595 (further noting that 'both the risk and urgency of the situation are acute ... The stability and resilience of our planet is in peril').

[192] See *supra* 1.1.2.

[193] Boyd (2019), p. 4.

[194] Ripple et al. (2020, 2021).

[195] World Meteorological Organization (2021) (noting that 2015–2021 are set to be the warmest 7 years on record, and sea level rise is at a new high).

[196] Trisos et al. (2020) (noting that 'a potentially catastrophic loss of global biodiversity is on the horizon'); IPBES (2019) (noting a rapid decline in biodiversity largely due to human actions).

[197] Ceballos et al. (2017); Ceballos et al. (2015); Barnosky et al. (2011).

interrelated public health risks such as the increasing emergence of zoonotic diseases like COVID-19.[198]

Evidently, all of these environmental problems are immediately and profoundly human rights-relevant.[199] Climate change is now widely recognized as an 'existential threat to civilization',[200] one of the biggest threats to humanity,[201] and among the greatest and most pressing threats to human rights of both living and future generations.[202] It already has major impacts on the full enjoyment of a wide range of human rights, such as the right to life (and in particular life with dignity),[203] health, food, water and sanitation, and is likely to have 'cataclysmic impact in the future' as the environmental crises worsen.[204] Climate-related natural disasters such as extreme weather events,[205] torrential rain and floods, heatwaves, wild fires, droughts, and rising sea-levels have dire humanitarian impacts,[206] and will lead to an increase in human mortality, illness, food and water insecurity,[207] mass climate

---

[198] Zoonotic diseases are natural threats that are exacerbated by environmental degradation. See IPBES (2020), p. 5 (noting that the 'underlying causes of pandemics are the same global environmental changes that drive biodiversity loss and climate change'); Barouki et al. (2021) (noting that the 'emergence and spread of SARS-CoV-2 appears to be related to urbanization, habitat destruction, live animal trade, intensive livestock farming and global travel').

[199] See Stucki et al. (2021).

[200] Lenton et al. (2019), p. 595.

[201] For an overview, see Wallace-Wells (2019) (noting that climate change is the 'biggest threat human life on the planet has ever faced', ibid., p. 6); Figueres and Rivett-Carnac (2020); Lieven (2020), p. 2ff.

[202] See Knox (2016), p. 7; CIEL (2019), p. 1 (noting that 'the climate crisis is the greatest-ever threat to human rights').

[203] See UN Human Rights Committee, General Comment No. 36, Article 6: Right to Life. 3 September 2019, CCPR/C/GC/36, para 62 (noting that 'Environmental degradation, climate change and unsustainable development constitute some of the most pressing and serious threats to the ability of present and future generations to enjoy the right to life . . . and in particular life with dignity'); two cases on climate change and the right to life are pending with the European Court of Human Rights. ECtHR, *Duarte Agostinho and Others v. Portugal and 32 Other States* (no. 39371/20); ECtHR, *Verein KlimaSeniorinnen Schweiz and Others v. Switzerland* (no. 53600/20); on the European Court of Human Rights' case law on the environment and Convention rights, see generally ECtHR, Factsheet – Environment and the ECHR (April 2021).

[204] See Boyd (2019), p. 10ff; Knox (2016), p. 7; Joint Statement on Human Rights and Climate Change by the Committee on the Elimination of Discrimination against Women, the Committee on Economic, Social and Cultural Rights, the Committee on the Protection of the Rights of All Migrant Workers and Members of Their Families, the Committee on the Rights of the Child and the Committee on the Rights of Persons with Disabilities, HRI/2019/1 (14 May 2020); CIEL (2019), p. 32 (noting that as 'the climate crisis worsens, so do the threats to the realization of human rights'); Lewis (2018), p. 15ff.

[205] See IPCC (2021), p. 10 (noting that anthropogenic climate change is already affecting the frequency and intensity of extreme weather in every region across the globe).

[206] See International Federation of Red Cross and Red Crescent Societies (2020).

[207] Oxfam (2021) (noting that climate change increases the frequency and intensity of extreme weather events and disasters such as storms, floods and droughts, which is one of the primary drivers of global hunger, food scarcity, and 'catastrophic food insecurity').

migration,[208] and resource conflicts.[209] Moreover, climate change and other environmental degradation act as an aggravator (the 'ultimate threat multiplier') of existing threats to international peace and security, and as a stressor to economic, social, and political systems and the stability of states, regions, and societies.[210] In short, the (human-made) natural crises of the Anthropocene threaten core aspects of human life, well-being, health, security, as well as society and humanity as a whole.

The existential environmental crises that humanity faces today are deeply interwoven with the institutionalized exploitation and extermination of animals that are part and parcel of our social and economic fabric.[211] Animal agriculture, especially industrial meat and milk production, is one of the main drivers (or the 'main culprit'[212]) of climate change and greenhouse gas emissions,[213] deforestation,[214] as well as biodiversity[215] and habitat loss.[216] Conversely, the need for transitioning to plant-based food systems and reducing the global consumption of animal products is now widely recognized—albeit not practiced—as a pivotal mitigation priority for halting climate change.[217] Moreover, the exploitation of farmed and wild animals exceedingly contributes to grave public health risks.[218] For example, three out of four emerging infectious diseases are zoonoses.[219] Wildlife markets (such as the one identified as a possible point of origin for the Corona virus)[220] and factory farms are

---

[208] Rigaud et al. (2018); UNHCR (2021).

[209] See Ekins et al. (2019), p. 47 (the pervasive effects of climate change include 'extreme events (including flooding, hurricanes and cyclones) leading to loss of lives and livelihoods, pervasive droughts leading to loss of agricultural productivity and food insecurity, severe heat waves, changes in disease vectors resulting in increases in morbidity and mortality, slowdowns in economic growth, and increased potentials for violent conflict').

[210] Rüttinger et al. (2015); Lieven (2020), p. 1ff.

[211] See generally Sebo (2022) (showing that human use of animals contributes to environmental, health, and other human-caused global threats); for a detailed exposition of the animals, pandemics, and climate change nexus, ibid., p. 40ff.

[212] Kivinen (2021), p. 197.

[213] The human activities with the largest climate impact are the burning of fossil fuels, deforestation, and industrial agriculture—and the latter two are intimately connected to animal production. See Ripple et al. (2017), p. 1026; Xu et al. (2021); FAO (2020).

[214] See WWF (2021), p. 5 (showing that the European Union is the World's second largest importer of tropical deforestation and associated greenhouse gas emissions, notably through its imports of agricultural commodities such as soy [used as livestock feed] and beef).

[215] See Benton et al. (2021) (identifying global food systems as a main driver of biodiversity loss).

[216] On animal agriculture's harmful environmental impacts, see generally FAO (2006).

[217] See only IPCC (2019), p. 488; European Commission (2021), p. 121f; Boyd (2019), p. 22; Sun et al. (2022); Philippidis et al. (2021); Ripple et al. (2020), p. 11; Clark et al. (2020); Willett et al. (2019); Springmann et al. (2018); Springmann et al. (2016), p. 4146.

[218] IPBES (2020), p. 5.

[219] See Coker et al. (2011), p. 326 (noting that 'nearly three-quarters of emerging and re-emerging diseases of human beings are zoonoses').

[220] Li et al. (2020).

breeding grounds for such zoonotic diseases that threaten human health.²²¹ Intensive animal farming, through its excessive use of antibiotics, also accelerates the rising threat of antimicrobial resistance. This growing public health problem is so serious, according to the WHO, that it 'threatens the achievements of modern medicine' and renders a 'post-antibiotic era … a very real possibility for the twenty-first century.'²²²

In short, our collective maltreatment of animals simultaneously causes, feeds into, and aggravates many of today's most pressing ecological risks to human rights. As Jeff Sebo encapsulates it, 'Our exploitation and extermination of nonhuman animals are not only harming many nonhuman animals but also contributing to public health threats such as pandemics and environmental threats such as climate change.'²²³

3.3.3.2 Indirect Contribution of Animal Rights towards Protecting Human Rights against Environmental Threats

Against the factual backdrop of ever-worsening environmental threats to human rights on the one hand and their intimate connection with our (ab)use and (mal)treatment of animals on the other hand, the eco-prudential argument for animal rights is as simple as it is compelling: animal rights would be beneficial to human rights, because eliminating animal exploitation will simultaneously eliminate one of the main drivers of some of the greatest human rights threats of our time.²²⁴

Contemporary human rights have an environmental dimension, and one increasingly important function of human rights is to protect humanity against the harms of climate change and other man-made natural threats.²²⁵ Human rights can properly fulfil this function only by addressing the underlying causes of these environmental risks and their nexus with animal exploitation, and by factoring in the interdependence of humans, animals, and the environment. In the natural sciences, this nexus is reflected in the concept of *One Health*—a holistic approach to global public health that recognizes the inextricable links between the health of humans,

---

²²¹ See Rabozzi et al. (2012), p. 77 (noting that 'animal breeding activities can pose a significant public health risk' with regard to emerging infectious diseases); Cascio et al. (2011), p. 336 (highlighting the human-related factors contributing to the resurgence of zoonoses, such as 'hunting or pet owning, and culinary habits, industrialization sequelae such as farming/food chain intensification, globalization of trade, human intrusion into ecosystems'); Rostal et al. (2013); IPBES (2020), p. 5 (noting that the 'underlying causes of pandemics are the same global environmental changes that drive biodiversity loss and climate change. These include land-use change, agricultural expansion and intensification, and wildlife trade and consumption').

²²² WHO (2014), p. IX; see also Rochford et al. (2018).

²²³ Sebo (2022), p. 117.

²²⁴ See also Sebo (2022), p. 6f (arguing that we need to include concern for animals as integral part of our climate change mitigation and adaption efforts).

²²⁵ See Knox (2021); Gross (2021).

(domestic and wild) animals, and the environment.[226] The central idea is that in order to achieve better public health outcomes for humans (for example, with regard to zoonotic diseases and antimicrobial resistance), it is necessary to integrate animal and environmental health, since these are interconnected.[227] This integrative strategy has been further extended to a *One Welfare* approach, which views human and animal welfare as 'intrinsically interconnected' and advocates 'balancing and promoting human and animal welfare in connected ecosystems and societies.'[228] The human–animal–environment nexus was further recognized in a recent United Nations Environment Assembly Resolution, noting that 'the health and welfare of animals, sustainable development and the environment are connected to human health and well-being' and acknowledging the 'increasing need to address these connections through the One Health approach, among other holistic approaches'.[229] Such a holistic approach—a *One Rights* approach—is also warranted in the realm of human rights, reflecting the environmentally mediated interdependence of humans and animals. Accordingly, the factual nexus between environmental human rights-threats and animal exploitation should translate to a normative nexus between protecting human and animal rights. Protecting human rights against environmental and health threats such as climate change and pandemics may be functionally best facilitated by integrating the protection of animals against precisely the kind of exploitation and extermination that contributes to those existential human rights threats.

Current environmental problems provide a compelling ecological rationale for abolishing our institutionalized exploitation of animals and (albeit only for instrumental reasons) vesting them with anti-exploitative rights, as an effective means of preserving the preconditions for the enjoyment of human rights. Ironically, or dialectically, our exploitation of animals has thus produced the very material conditions that now render it prudent to recognize animal rights as an integral part of the human rights mandate. Simply put, treating animals as if they mattered (even if we cannot agree on the moral foundations) seems to be the best institutional safeguard against some of the worst environmental threats humanity faces today. Addressing the animal question is thus far from a mere ethical issue, but rather, it has become an

---

[226] See e.g. Rostal et al. (2013), p. 102 ('One Health is the all-encompassing concept that recognizes the inextricable links between the health of people, animals (wild and domestic), and the environment'); Atlas (2013), p. 1f; on One Health, see generally Mackenzie et al. (2013); Zinsstag et al. (2021).

[227] For example, the World Health Organization (WHO), Food and Agriculture Organization (FAO), and World Organisation for Animal Health (OIE) have established, under the One Health approach, a 'formal tripartite alliance to enhance global coordination and to promote intersectoral collaboration between the public health and animal health sectors as well as in food safety'. WHO (2014), p. 62.

[228] Colonius and Earley (2013); García Pinillos (2018), p. 12 (defining One Welfare as 'a collaborative approach for integrating animal welfare, human wellbeing and the environment, with an end point of improving global welfare').

[229] United Nations Environment Assembly, Resolution on the Animal Welfare-Environment-Sustainable Development Nexus, adopted on 2 March 2022, UNEP/EA.5/L.10/Rev.1.

existential necessity for humans. While it is sometimes assumed that the idea of animal rights is a nicety we can tend to once human rights are fully realized and secured, this belief is fatally mistaken. Quite the opposite is true: in the face of mounting environmental crises, ignoring the animal question has become a luxury humanity can no longer afford.

In the end, human and animal rights are in the same boat. Contrary to the antagonistic intuition, however, this metaphor does not stand for a lifeboat scenario[230] in which animals have to be sacrificed in order to save human rights, but for a situation of shared fate and interdependence. Because human and animal existence are naturally and evermore interdependent, so should be the rights protecting them—One Health, One Welfare, One Rights.

References

Abbey R (2017) Closer kinships: Rortyan resources for animal rights. Contemp Polit Theory 16:1–18

Adams CJ (2007) The war on compassion. In: Donovan J, Adams CJ (eds) The feminist care tradition in animal ethics: a reader. Columbia University Press, New York, pp 21–36

Adams CJ (2013) The sexual politics of meat: a feminist-vegetarian critical theory, 20th Anniversary edn. Bloomsbury, New York

Adams CJ, Donovan J (eds) (1995) Animals and women: feminist theoretical explorations. Duke University Press, Durham

Adams CJ, Gruen L (eds) (2014) Ecofeminism: feminist intersections with other animals & the earth. Bloomsbury, New York

Adorno T (2005) Minima Moralia: reflections from damaged life. Verso, London/New York

Arluke A, Levin J, Luke C, Ascione F (1999) The relationship of animal abuse to violence and other forms of antisocial behavior. J Interpers Violence 14:963–975

Atlas RM (2013) One health: its origins and future. In: Mackenzie JS, Jeggo M, Daszak P, Richt JA (eds) One health: the human-animal-environment interfaces in emerging infectious diseases. Springer, Heidelberg, pp 1–13

Bailey C (2009) A man and a dog in a lifeboat: self-sacrifice, animals, and the limits of ethical theory. Ethics Environ 14:129–148

Barnosky AD et al (2011) Has the earth's sixth mass extinction already arrived? Nature 471:51–57

Barouki R et al (2021) The COVID-19 pandemic and global environmental change: emerging research needs. Environ Int 146:106272

Bastian B, Costello K, Loughnan S, Hodson G (2012) When closing the human-animal divide expands moral concern: the importance of framing. Soc Psychol Personal Sci 3:421–429

Beirne P (2004) From animal abuse to interhuman violence? A critical review of the progression thesis. Soc Anim 12:39–65

Beirne P (2009) Confronting animal abuse: Law, criminology, and human-animal relationships. Rowman & Littlefield, Lanham

---

[230] The hypothetical lifeboat scenario in which either the human or the animal has to be sacrificed. See e.g. Regan (2004), p. 324f; for a critical take on these hypotheticals, see Donovan (1990), p. 375 (noting that 'In most cases, either/or dilemmas in real life can be turned into both/ands. In most cases, dead-end situations such as those posed in lifeboat hypotheticals can be prevented'); Bailey (2009).

Beitz CR (2004) Human rights and the Law of peoples. In: Chatterjee DK (ed) The ethics of assistance: morality and the distant needy. Cambridge University Press, Cambridge, pp 193–214

Beitz CR (2009) The idea of human rights. Oxford University Press, Oxford

Bentham J (1789) An introduction to the principles of morals and legislation. T Payne & Son, London

Benton T (1993) Natural relations: ecology, animal rights and social justice. Verso, London

Benton TG, Bieg C, Harwatt H, Pudasaini R, Wellesley L (2021) Food system impacts on biodiversity loss: three levers for food system transformation in support of nature. Research Paper, Chatham House

Besson S (2012) Human rights: ethical, political... or legal? First steps in a legal theory of human rights. In: Childress DE III (ed) The role of ethics in international Law. Cambridge University Press, Cambridge, pp 211–245

Besson S (2015) Human rights and constitutional Law: patterns of mutual validation and legitimation. In: Cruft R, Liao SM, Renzo M (eds) Philosophical foundations of human rights. Oxford University Press, Oxford, pp 279–299

Besson S (2018) Justifications. In: Moeckli D, Shah S, Sivakumaran S (eds) International human rights law, 3rd edn. Oxford University Press, Oxford, pp 22–40

Bilchitz D (2009) Moving beyond arbitrariness: the legal personhood and dignity of non-human animals. South Afr J Human Rights 25:38–72

Bilchitz D (2010) Does transformative constitutionalism require the recognition of animal rights? South Afr Public Law 25:267–300

Bilchitz D (2018) Fundamental rights as bridging concepts: straddling the boundary between ideal justice and an imperfect reality. Hum Rights Q 40:119–143

Birke L (2000) Supporting the underdog: feminism, animal rights and citizenship in the work of Alice Morgan Wright and Edith Goode. Women's Hist Rev 9:693–719

Bob C (2009) Introduction: fighting for new rights. In: Bob C (ed) The international struggle for new human rights. University of Pennsylvania Press, Philadelphia, pp 1–13

Bobbio N (1996) The age of rights (trans: Cameron A). Polity Press, Cambridge

Boggs CG (2010) American bestiality: sex, animals, and the construction of subjectivity. Cult Crit 76:98–125

Boyd DR (2019) Human Rights obligations relating to the enjoyment of a safe, clean, healthy and sustainable environment: report of the special Rapporteur on human rights and the environment. 19 July 2019, A/74/161

Brown W (2004) 'The Most we can Hope for...': human rights and the politics of fatalism. South Atlantic Q 103:451–463

Bryant TL (2010) Denying animals childhood and its implications for animal-protective Law reform. Law Cult Human 6:56–74

Bucchieri RL (2016) Bridging the gap: the connection between violence against animals and violence against humans. J Anim Nat Res Law 11:115–136

Cao D (2014) Crimes against animality: animal cruelty and criminal justice in a globalized world. In: Arrigo BA, Bersot HY (eds) Routledge handbook of international crime and justice studies. Routledge, pp 169–190

Casal P (2003) Is multiculturalism bad for animals? J Polit Philos 11:1–22

Cascio A, Bosilkovski M, Rodriguez-Morales AJ, Pappas G (2011) The socio-ecology of zoonotic infections. Clin Microbiol Infect 17:336–342

Cavalieri P (2001) The animal question: why nonhuman animals deserve human rights. Oxford University Press, Oxford

Ceballos G, Ehrlich PR, Barnosky AD, García A, Pringle RM, Palmer TM (2015) Accelerated modern human-induced species losses: entering the sixth mass extinction. Sci Adv 1(5): e1400253

Ceballos G, Ehrlich PR, Dirzo R (2017) Biological annihilation via the ongoing sixth mass extinction signaled by vertebrate population losses and declines. PNAS 114(30):E6089–E6096

References

CIEL Center for International Environmental Law (2019) Rights in a Changing Climate: Human Rights Under the UN Framework Convention on Climate Change

Clark MA et al (2020) Global food system emissions could preclude achieving the 1.5° and 2°C climate change targets. Science 370:705–708

Clough DL (2018) On animals, Volume II: theological ethics. T&T Clark, London

Cochrane A (2013) From human rights to sentient rights. Crit Rev Int Soc Pol Phil 16:655–675

Cochrane A (2018) Sentientist politics: a theory of global inter-species justice. Oxford University Press, Oxford

Cohen J (2004) Minimalism about human rights: the Most we can Hope for? J Polit Philos 12:190–213

Coker R et al (2011) Towards a conceptual framework to support one-Health Research for policy on emerging zoonoses. Lancet Infect Dis 11:326–331

Colling S (2020) Animal resistance in the global capitalist era. Michigan State University Press, East Lansing

Colonius TJ, Earley RW (2013) One welfare: a call to develop a broader framework of thought and action. J Am Vet Med Assoc 242:309–310

Costello K, Hodson G (2010) Exploring the roots of dehumanization: the role of animal-human similarity in promoting immigrant humanization. Group Process Intergroup Relat 13:3–22

Costello K, Hodson G (2014) Explaining dehumanization among children: the interspecies model of prejudice. Br J Soc Psychol 53:175–197

Coulter K (2016) Animals, work, and the promise of interspecies solidarity. Palgrave Macmillan, Basingstoke

Cruft R, Liao SM, Renzo M (2015) The philosophical foundations of human rights: an overview. In: Cruft R, Liao SM, Renzo M (eds) Philosophical foundations of human rights. Oxford University Press, Oxford, pp 1–41

Cudworth E (2015) Killing animals: sociology, species relations and institutionalized violence. Sociol Rev 63:1–18

Cupp RL (2009) Moving beyond animal rights: a legal/contractualist critique. San Diego Law Rev 46:27–84

D'Amato A, Chopra SK (1991) Whales: their emerging right to life. Am J Int Law 85:21–62

Darwin C (1871) The descent of man, and selection in relation to sex, vol I. John Murray, London

Deckha M (2012) Critical animal studies and animal law. Anim Law 18:207–236

DeCoux EL (2009) Speaking for the modern prometheus: the significance of animal suffering to the abolition movement. Anim Law 16:9–64

DeMello M (2012) Animals and society: an introduction to human-animal studies. Columbia University Press, New York

Dershowitz A (2004) Rights from wrongs: a secular theory of the origins of rights. Basic Books, New York

Dhont K, Hodson G, Costello K, MacInnis CC (2014) Social dominance orientation connects prejudicial human-human and human-animal relations. Personal Individ Differ 61–62:105–108

Donaldson S, Kymlicka W (2007) The Moral Ark. Queen's Q 114:187–205

Donaldson S, Kymlicka W (2011) Zoopolis: a political theory of animal rights. Oxford University Press, Oxford

Donnelly J (2013) Universal human rights in theory and practice, 3rd edn. Cornell University Press, Ithaca

Donovan J (1990) Animal rights and feminist theory. Signs 15:350–375

Donovan J (2007) Attention to suffering: sympathy as a basis for ethical treatment of animals. In: Donovan J, Adams CJ (eds) The feminist care tradition in animal ethics. Columbia University Press, New York, pp 174–197

Donovan J, Adams CJ (eds) (1996) Beyond animal rights: a feminist caring ethic for the treatment of animals. Continuum, New York

Douzinas C (2000) The end of human rights: critical legal thought at the turn of the century. Hart, Oxford

Dubeau M (2020) Species-being for whom? The five faces of interspecies oppression. Contemp Polit Theory 19:596–620

Ekins P, Gupta J, Boileau P (eds) (2019) Global environment outlook GEO-6: healthy planet, healthy people. Cambridge University Press/UN Environment, Cambridge/Nairobi

European Commission (2021) Proposal for a Regulation of the European Parliament and of the Council on Land Use, Forestry, and Agriculture, COM(2021) 554 final (14 July 2021)

FAO (2020) Agriculture and climate change: law and governance in support of climate smart agriculture and international climate change goals, FAO legislative studies no 115. FAO, Rome

FAO Food and Agriculture Organization (2006) Livestock's long shadow: environmental issues and options. FAO, Rome

Fasel RN (2019) More equal than others: animals in the age of human rights aristocracy, PhD thesis. University of Cambridge

Faver CA, Strand EB (2003) Domestic violence and animal cruelty: untangling the web of abuse. J Soc Work Educ 39:237–253

Feinberg J (1973) Social philosophy. Prentice-Hall, Englewood Cliffs

Feinberg J (1992) In defence of moral rights. Oxf J Leg Stud 12:149–169

Figueres C & Rivett-Carnac T (2020) The future we choose: surviving the climate crisis. Alfred A. Knopf, New York

Fox M (2004) Re-thinking kinship: Law's construction of the animal body. Curr Leg Probl 57:469–493

Francione GL (1995) Animals, property, and the law (reprinted 2007 with corrections). Temple University Press, Philadelphia

Francione GL (2000) Introduction to animal rights: your child or the dog? Temple University Press, Philadelphia

Francione GL (2020) Some brief comments on animal rights. Anim Front 10:29–33

Fromm E (1973) The anatomy of human destructiveness. Holt, Rinehart and Winston, New York/Chicago

Gaard G (ed) (1993a) Ecofeminism: women, animals, nature. Temple University Press, Philadelphia

Gaard G (1993b) Living interconnections with animals and nature. In: Gaard G (ed) Ecofeminism: women, animals, nature. Temple University Press, Philadelphia, pp 1–12

Gaarder E (2011) Women and the animal rights movement. Rutgers University Press, New Brunswick

García Pinillos R (2018) One welfare: a framework to improve animal welfare and human wellbeing. CABI, Wallingford

Gearty C (2009) Is human rights Speciesist? In: Linzey A (ed) The link between animal abuse and human violence. Sussex Academic Press, Brighton/Portland, pp 175–183

Gearty C (2010) Do human rights help or hinder environmental protection? J Human Rights Environ 1:7–22

Golder B (2016) Theorizing human rights. In: Orford A, Hoffmann F (eds) Oxford handbook of the theory of international law. Oxford University Press, Oxford, pp 684–700

Gross T (2021) Climate change and duties to protect with regard to fundamental rights. In: Kahl W, Weller MP (eds) Climate change litigation: a handbook. Beck, München, pp 82–97

Gruen L (1996) On the oppression of women and animals. Environ Ethics 18:441–444

Gruen L (2009) The faces of animal oppression. In: Ferguson A, Nagel M (eds) Dancing with iris: the philosophy of iris Marion young. Oxford University Press, Oxford, pp 161–172

Gruen L (2015) Entangled empathy: an alternative ethic for our relationships with animals. Lantern Books, New York

Harari Yuval Noah (2015) Industrial farming is one of the worst crimes in history. The Guardian, 25 September 2015. https://www.theguardian.com/books/2015/sep/25/industrial-farming-one-worst-crimes-history-ethical-question

Harvey P (2004) Aspirational law. Buffalo Law Rev 52:701–726

Haslam N (2006) Dehumanization: an integrative review. Personal Soc Psychol Rev 10:252–264

Haslam N (2014) What is dehumanization? In: Bain PG, Vaes J, Leyens J-P (eds) Humanness and dehumanization. Routledge, New York, pp 34–48

Haslam N, Loughnan S, Reynolds C, Wilson S (2007) Dehumanization: a new perspective. Soc Personal Psychol Compass 1(1):409–422

Hetey RC, Eberhardt JL (2014) Cops and criminals: the interplay of mechanistic and animalistic dehumanization in the criminal justice system. In: Bain PG, Vaes J, Leyens J-P (eds) Humanness and dehumanization. Routledge, New York, pp 147–166

Hodson G, MacInnis CC, Costello K (2014) (over)valuing 'Humanness' as an aggravator of intergroup prejudices and discrimination. In: Bain PG, Vaes J, Leyens J-P (eds) Humanness and dehumanization. Routledge, New York, pp 86–110

Hoffmann FF (2006) 'Shooting into the dark': toward a pragmatic theory of human rights (activism). Tex In Law J 41:403–414

Horta O, Albersmeier F (2020) Defining speciesism. Philosophy Compass 15(11):1–9. https://doi.org/10.1111/phc3.12708

Hribal J (2010) Fear of the animal planet: the hidden history of animal resistance. AK Press, Chico

Hunt L (2007) Inventing human rights: a history. W.W. Norton & Company, New York

Ignatieff M (2001) Human rights as politics and idolatry. In: Gutmann A (ed) Human rights as politics and idolatry. Princeton University Press, Princeton, pp 3–98

International Federation of Red Cross and Red Crescent Societies (2020) World disasters report 2020, come heat or high water: tackling the humanitarian impacts of the climate crisis together. IFRC, Geneva

IPBES (2019) In: Brondizio ES, Settele J, Díaz S, Ngo HT (eds) Global assessment report on biodiversity and ecosystem services of the intergovernmental science-policy platform on biodiversity and ecosystem services. IPBES Secretariat, Bonn

IPBES (2020) IPBES workshop on biodiversity and pandemics: executive summary. IPBES Secretariat, Bonn

IPCC (2019) Climate Change and Land: an IPCC special report on climate change, desertification, land degradation, sustainable land management, food security, and greenhouse gas fluxes in terrestrial ecosystems. In: Shukla PR, Skea J, Calvo Buendia E, Masson-Delmotte V, Pörtner H-O, Roberts DC, Zhai P, Slade R, Connors S, van Diemen R, Ferrat M, Haughey E, Luz S, Neogi S, Pathak M, Petzold J, Portugal Pereira J, Vyas P, Huntley E, Kissick K, Belkacemi M, Malley J, (eds)

IPCC (2021) Climate change 2021: the physical science basis. Cambridge University Press, Cambridge

Jenkins S, Stanescu V (2014) One struggle. In: Nocella AJ II, Sorenson J, Socha K, Matsuoka A (eds) Defining critical animal studies: an intersectional social justice approach for liberation. Peter Lang, New York, pp 74–85

Jones RC (2015) Animal rights is a social justice issue. Contemp Just Rev 18:467–482

Karp DJ (2020) What is the responsibility to respect human rights? Reconsidering the 'respect, protect, and fulfill' framework. Int Theory 12:83–108

Keim S, Sosnowski J (2012) Human rights v animal rights: mutually exclusive or complementary causes? Aust Anim Protect Law J 8:78–83

Kemmerer L (ed) (2011) Sister species: women, animals, and social justice. University of Illinois Press, Champaign

Kivinen T (2021) Animal rights and rhetorical topoi. Scand Stud Law 67:179–202

Knight A, Watson KD (2017) Was Jack the ripper a slaughterman? Human-animal violence and the world's most infamous serial killer. Animals 7(4):1–30. https://doi.org/10.3390/ani7040030

Knowles LP (2001) The lingua Franca of human rights and the rise of a global bioethic. Camb Q Healthc Ethics 10:253–263

Knox JH (2016) Report of the Special Rapporteur on the Issue of Human Rights Obligations Relating to the Enjoyment of a Safe, Clean, Healthy and Sustainable Environment. 1 February 2016, A/HRC/31/52

Knox JH (2021) Human rights. In: Rajamani L, Peel J (eds) Oxford handbook of international environmental law, 2nd edn. Oxford University Press, Oxford, pp 784–799

Korsgaard CM (2009) Exploiting animals: a philosophical protest. AV Magazine 117(4):14–15

Korsgaard CM (2018) Fellow creatures: our obligations to the other animals. Oxford University Press, Oxford

Koskenniemi M (2010) Human rights mainstreaming as a strategy for institutional power. Humanity 1:47–58

Kreide R (2015) Human rights as placeholders. Fudan J Human Soc Sci 8:401–413

Kundera M (1999) The unbearable lightness of being (transl. Michael Henry Heim). Faber and Faber, London

Kymlicka W (2017) Social membership: animal law beyond the property/personhood impasse. Dalhousie Law J 40:123–155

Kymlicka W (2018) Human rights without human supremacism. Can J Philos 48:763–792

Kymlicka W, Donaldson S (2014) Animal rights, multiculturalism, and the left. J Soc Philos 45:116–135

Kymlicka W, Donaldson S (2016) Locating animals in political philosophy. Philos Compass 11:692–701

Kymlicka W, Donaldson S (2018) Rights. In: Gruen L (ed) Critical terms for animal studies. University of Chicago Press, Chicago, pp 320–336

Langlois AJ (2016) Normative and theoretical foundations of human rights. In: Goodhart M (ed) Human rights: politics and practice, 3rd edn. Oxford University Press, Oxford, pp 11–27

Lenton TM, Rockström J, Gaffney O, Rahmstorf S, Richardson K, Steffen W, Schellnhuber HJ (2019) Climate tipping points – too risky to bet against. Nature 575:592–595

Lewis B (2018) Environmental human rights and climate change: current status and future prospects. Springer, Singapore

Li Q et al (2020) Early transmission dynamics in Wuhan, China, of novel coronavirus-infected pneumonia. N Engl J Med 382:1199–1207

Liao SM, Etinson A (2012) Political and naturalistic conceptions of human rights: a false polemic? J Moral Philos 9:327–352

Lieven A (2020) Climate change and the nation state: the realist case. Allen Lane, London

Linzey A (ed) (2009) The link between animal abuse and human violence. Sussex Academic Press, Brighton

Livingstone Smith D (2011) Less than human: why we demean, enslave, and exterminate others. St. Martin's Press, New York

Lorite Escorihuela A (2011) A global slaughterhouse. Helsinki Rev Glob Gov 2:25–29

Lucia S, Killias M (2011) Is animal cruelty a marker of interpersonal violence and delinquency? Results of a Swiss National Self-Report Study. Psychol Violence 1:93–105

MacCormick N (2008) Institutions of law: an essay in legal theory. Oxford University Press, Oxford

Mackenzie JS, Jeggo M, Daszak P, Richt JA (eds) (2013) One health: the human-animal-environment interfaces in emerging infectious diseases. Springer, Heidelberg

MacKinnon CA (1993) Toward feminist jurisprudence. In: Smith P (ed) Feminist Jurisprudence. Oxford University Press, Oxford, pp 610–619

MacKinnon CA (2005) Of mice and men: a feminist fragment on animal rights. In: Sunstein CR, Nussbaum MC (eds) Animal rights: current debates and new directions. Oxford University Press, Oxford, pp 263–276

Maher J, Pierpoint H, Beirne P (eds) (2017) The Palgrave international handbook of animal abuse studies. Palgrave Macmillan, London

Marceau J (2019) Beyond cages: animal law and criminal punishment. Cambridge University Press, Cambridge

Marcuse H (1965) Repressive tolerance. In: Wolff RP, Moore B Jr, Marcuse H (eds) A critique of pure tolerance. Beacon Press, Boston

Matsuoka A, Sorenson J (2013) Human consequences of animal exploitation: needs for redefining social welfare. J Sociol Soc Welf 40(4):7–32

Nagan WP, Cartner JAC, Munro RJ (2016) Human rights and dynamic humanism. Brill Nijhoff, Leiden
National Sheriffs' Association (2018) Animal Cruelty as a Gateway Crime. U.S. Department of Justice, Office of Community Oriented Policing Services, Washington
Nelson L (1949) System der philosophischen Ethik und Pädagogik (aus dem Nachlass herausgegeben von Grete Hermann und Minna Specht, 2. unveränderte Auflage). Meiner, Hamburg
Nelson L (1972) Lebensnähe (1926). In: Nelson L, Recht und Staat: Gesammelte Schriften in neun Bänden, Band 9. Felix Meiner Verlag, Hamburg
Neuman GL (2003) Human rights and constitutional rights: harmony and dissonance. Stanford Law Rev 55:1863–1900
Nibert D (2002) Animal rights/human rights: entanglements of oppression and liberation. Rowman & Littlefield, Lanham
Nibert DA (1994) Animal rights and human social issues. Soc Anim 2:115–124
Nibert DA (2013) Animal oppression and human violence: domesecration, capitalism, and global conflict. Columbia University Press, New York
Nickel JW (2007) Making sense of human rights, 2nd edn. Blackwell, Malden
Niesen P (2020) Erst Ethik, dann Politik, oder: Politik statt Ethik? Zur Grundlegung der Tierrechte im *political turn*. TIERethik 12(2):7–28
Nocella AJ II, Sorenson J, Socha K, Matsuoka A (eds) (2014) Defining critical animal studies: an intersectional social justice approach for liberation. Peter Lang, New York
Norwood FB, Lusk JL (2011) Compassion, by the pound: the economics of farm animal welfare. Oxford University Press, Oxford
Nurse A (2016) An introduction to green criminology & environmental justice. SAGE, London
Nussbaum MC (2005) Beyond 'compassion and humanity': justice for nonhuman animals. In: Sunstein CR, Nussbaum MC (eds) Animal rights: current debates and new directions. Oxford University Press, Oxford, pp 299–320
Nussbaum MC (2018) Working with and for animals: getting the theoretical framework right. J Human Dev Capabil 19:2–18
Nussbaum MC (2022) Justice for animals: our collective responsibility. Simon & Schuster, New York
Oxfam (2021) The Hunger Virus Multiplies: Deadly Recipe of Conflict, COVID-19 and Climate Accelerate World Hunger. Oxfam Media Briefing (9 July 2021)
Park YS, Valentino B (2019) Animals are people too: explaining variation in respect for animal rights. Hum Rights Q 41:39–65
Patterson C (2002) Eternal Treblinka: our treatment of animals and the holocaust. Lantern Books, New York
Peters A (2016) Liberté, Égalité, Animalité: human-animal comparisons in law. Transnatl Environ Law 5:25–53
Peters A (2018) Rights of human and nonhuman animals: complementing the universal declaration of human rights. AJIL Unbound 112:355–360
Peters A (2021a) The importance of having rights. Heidelberg J Int Law 81:7–22
Peters A (2021b) Animals in international law. Pocketbooks of the Hague Academy of International Law. Brill/Nijhoff, Leiden
Philippidis G, Ferrer-Pérez H, Gracia-de-Rentería P, M'barek R, Sanjuán López AI (2021) Eating your greens: a global sustainability assessment. Resour Conserv Recycl 168 105460
Pleasants N (2008) Structure and agency in the antislavery and animal liberation movements. In: Muers R, Grumett D (eds) Eating and believing: interdisciplinary perspectives on vegetarianism and theology. T&T Clark, London, pp 198–216
Plous S (2003) Is there such a thing as prejudice toward animals? In: Plous S (ed) Understanding prejudice and discrimination. McGraw-Hill, New York, pp 509–528
Pocar V (1992) Animal rights: a socio-legal perspective. J Law Soc 19:214–230

Posner R (2006) Animal rights: legal, philosophical and pragmatic perspectives. In: Sunstein CR, Nussbaum MC (eds) Animal rights: current debates and new directions. Oxford University Press, New York, pp 50–77

Rabozzi G et al (2012) Emerging zoonoses: the 'one health approach'. Saf Health Work 3:77–83

Rawls J (1993) The law of peoples. Crit Inq 20:36–68

Rawls J (1999) The law of peoples. Harvard University Press, Cambridge, Mass./London

Raz J (2010) Human rights without foundations. In: Besson S, Tasioulas J (eds) The philosophy of international Law. Oxford University Press, Oxford, pp 321–337

Regan T (1985) The case for animal rights. In: Singer P (ed) In defense of animals. Basil Blackwell, New York, pp 13–26

Regan T (2004) The case for animal rights, updated with a new preface. University of California Press, Berkeley

Rigaud K et al (2018) Groundswell: preparing for internal climate migration. The World Bank, Washington, DC

Ripple WJ, Wolf C, Newsome TM, Galetti M, Alamgir M, Crist E, Mahmoud MI, Laurance WF and 15'364 Scientists Signatories from 184 Countries (2017) World scientists' warning to humanity: a second notice. Bioscience 67:1026–1028

Ripple WJ, Wolf C, Newsome TM, Barnard P, Moomaw WR, and 11'258 Scientist Signatories from 153 Countries (2020) World scientists' warning of a climate emergency. Bioscience 70:8–12

Ripple WJ, Wolf C, Newsome TM, Gregg JW, Lenton TM, Palomo I, Eikelboom JAJ, Law BE, Huq S, Duffy PB, Rockström J (2021) World scientists' warning of a climate emergency 2021. Bioscience 71:894–898

Rochford C et al (2018) Global governance of antimicrobial resistance. Lancet 391:1976–1978

Rorty R (1993) Human rights, rationality, and sentimentality. In: Shute S, Hurley S (eds) On human rights: the Oxford amnesty lectures. Basic Books, New York, pp 111–134

Rorty R (1999) Philosophy and social hope. Penguin Books, London

Rostal MK, Olival KJ, Loh EH, Karesh WB (2013) Wildlife: the need to better understand the linkages. In: Mackenzie JS, Jeggo M, Daszak P, Richt JA (eds) One health: the human-animal-environment interfaces in emerging infectious diseases. Springer, Heidelberg, pp 101–125

Rowlands M (2002) Animals like us. Verso Books, London

Roylance C, Abeyta AA, Routledge C (2016) I am not an animal but I am a sexist: human distinctiveness, sexist attitudes towards women, and perceptions of meaning in life. Fem Psychol 26:368–377

Rüttinger L, Smith D, Stang G, Tänzler D & Vivekananda J (2015) A new climate for peace: taking action on climate and fragility risks. An Independent Report Commissioned by the G7 Members

Safran Foer J (2009) Eating animals. Back Bay Books, New York

Salt HS (1894) Animals' rights considered in relation to social progress. Macmillan, New York

Sankoff P (2013) The protection paradigm: making the world a better place for animals? In: Sankoff P, White S, Black C (eds) Animal law in Australasia: continuing the dialogue, 2nd edn. Federation Press, Sydney, pp 1–30

Schmahmann DR, Polacheck LJ (1995) The case against rights for animals. Environ Aff Law Rev 22:747–781

Schulz WF, Raman S (2020) The coming good society: why new realities demand new rights. Harvard University Press, Cambridge

Scully M (2003) Dominion: the power of man, the suffering of animals, and the call to mercy. St. Martin's Griffin, New York

Sebo J (2022) Saving animals, saving ourselves: why animals matter for pandemics, climate change, and other catastrophes. Oxford University Press, Oxford

Sen A (2004) Elements of a theory of human rights. Philos Public Aff 32:315–356

Shue H (1996) Basic rights: subsistence, affluence, and U.S. foreign policy, 2nd edn. Princeton University Press, Princeton

Silverstein H (1996) Unleashing rights: law, meaning, and the animal rights movement. University of Michigan Press, Ann Arbor

Skorupski J (2010) Human rights. In: Besson S, Tasioulas J (eds) The philosophy of international law. Oxford University Press, Oxford, pp 357–373

Spiegel M (1996) The dreaded comparison: human and animal slavery. Mirror Books, New York

Springmann M, Godfray HCJ, Rayner M, Scarborough P (2016) Analysis and valuation of the health and climate change cobenefits of dietary change. Proc Natl Acad Sci USA 113:4146–4151

Springmann M et al (2018) Options for keeping the food system within environmental limits. Nature 562:519–525

Stache C (2020) Conceptualising animal exploitation in capitalism: getting terminology straight. Cap Class 44:401–421

Stone A (2022) The relationship between attitudes to human rights and to animal rights is partially mediated by empathy. J Soc Psychol:1–14. https://doi.org/10.1080/00224545.2022.2140024

Stucki S (2016) Grundrechte für Tiere. Nomos, Baden-Baden

Stucki S (2020) Towards a theory of legal animal rights: simple and fundamental rights. Oxf J Leg Stud 40:533–560

Stucki S (2023) Animal warfare law and the need for an animal law of peace: a comparative reconstruction. Am J Comp Law 71 (forthcoming)

Stucki S et al (2021) World lawyers' pledge on climate action. Environ Policy Law 51:371–376

Sun Z, Scherer L, Tukker A, Spawn-Lee SA, Bruckner M, Gibbs HK, Behrens P (2022) Dietary change in high-income nations alone can lead to substantial double climate dividend. Nat Food 3:29–37

Susi M (2020) Novelty in new human rights: the decrease in universality and abstractness thesis. In: von Arnauld A, von der Decken K, Susi M (eds) Cambridge handbook of new human rights: recognition, novelty, rhetoric. Cambridge University Press, Cambridge, pp 21–33

Sykes K (2011) Nations like unto yourselves: an inquiry into the status of a general principle of international Law on animal welfare. Canadian Yearb Int Law 49:3–50

Sztybel D (2006) Can the treatment of animals be compared to the holocaust? Ethics Environ 11:97–132

Taylor A (2010) Review of Wesley J Smith's a rat is a pig is a dog is a boy: the human cost of the animal rights movement. Between Spec 10:223–236

Traïni C (2016) The animal rights struggle: an essay in historical sociology. Amsterdam University Press, Amsterdam

Trisos CH, Merow C, Pigot AL (2020) The projected timing of abrupt ecological disruption from climate change. Nature 580:496–501

UNHCR (2021) Global Trends: Forced Displacement in 2020. United Nations High Commissioner for Refugees

Upadhya V (2014) The abuse of animals as a method of domestic violence: the need for criminalization. Emory Law J 63:1163–1209

Valentini L (2017) Dignity and human rights: a reconceptualisation. Oxf J Leg Stud 37:862–885

Veser P, Taylor K, Singer S (2015) Diet, authoritarianism, social dominance orientation, and predisposition to prejudice. Br Food J 117:1949–1960

von Arnauld A, Theilen JT (2020) Rhetoric of rights: a topical perspective on the functions of claiming a 'human right to...'. In: von Arnauld A, von der Decken K, Susi M (eds) Cambridge handbook of new human rights: recognition, novelty, rhetoric. Cambridge University Press, Cambridge, pp 34–49

von Harbou F (2014) The natural faculty of empathy as a basis for human rights. In: Albers M, Hoffmann T, Reinhardt J (eds) Human rights and human nature. Springer, Dordrecht, pp 95–108

Wadiwel DJ (2015) The war against animals. Brill, Leiden

Wallace-Wells D (2019) The uninhabitable earth: a story of the future. Penguin Books, London

Weinbren D (1994) Against all cruelty: the humanitarian league, 1891–1919. Hist Work J 38:86–105

Weitzenfeld A, Joy M (2014) An overview of anthropocentrism, humanism, and speciesism in critical animal theory. In: Nocella AJ II, Sorenson J, Socha K, Matsuoka A (eds) Defining

critical animal studies: an intersectional social justice approach for liberation. Peter Lang, New York, pp 3–27
White S, Cao D (2016) Introduction: animal protection in an interconnected world. In: Cao D, White S (eds) Animal Law and welfare – international perspectives. Springer, Cham, pp 1–7
WHO World Health Organization (2014) Antimicrobial resistance: global report on surveillance. WHO, Geneva
Willett W et al (2019) Food in the Anthropocene: the EAT-lancet commission on healthy diets from sustainable food systems. Lancet Commissions 393:447–492
Williams PJ (1987) Alchemical notes: reconstructing ideals from deconstructed rights. Harv Civil Rights-Civil Libert Law Rev 22:401–434
Wills J (2018) Expanding the Moral Circle to Nonhuman Animals. Juriosity, 13 December 2018. https://www.juriosity.com/knowledge/article/485f4484-492c-4568-afae-ae2bcb81ad75
Wills J (2020) Animal rights, legal personhood and cognitive capacity: addressing 'levelling-down' concerns. J Human Rights Environ 11:199–223
Winston M (2007) Human rights as moral rebellion and social construction. J Human Rights 6:279–305
Wise SM (1998) Hardly a revolution: the eligibility of nonhuman animals for dignity-rights in a Liberal democracy. Vermont Law Rev 22:793–916
Wise SM (2000) Rattling the cage: toward legal rights for animals. Basic Books, New York
Wolfe C (2003) Animal rites: American culture, the discourse of species, and Posthumanist theory. University of Chicago Press, Chicago
Wolfe C (2013) Before the Law: humans and other animals in a biopolitical frame. University of Chicago Press, Chicago
World Meteorological Organization (2021) State of climate in 2021: extreme events and major impacts. WMO, Geneva
WWF (2021) Stepping Up? The Continuing Impact of EU Consumption on Nature Worldwide: Summary Report
Xu X, Sharma P, Shu S, Lin TS, Ciais P, Tubiello FN, Smith P, Campbell N, Jain AK (2021) Global greenhouse gas emissions from animal-based foods are twice those of plant-based foods. Nat Food 2:724–732
Zinsstag J, Schelling E, Crump L, Whittaker M, Tanner M, Stephen C (eds) (2021) One health: the theory and practice of integrated health approaches, 2nd edn. CABI, Wallingford
Zuolo F (2020) Cooperation with animals? What is and what is not. J Agric Environ Ethics 33:315–335

Open Access This chapter is licensed under the terms of the Creative Commons Attribution 4.0 International License (http://creativecommons.org/licenses/by/4.0/), which permits use, sharing, adaptation, distribution and reproduction in any medium or format, as long as you give appropriate credit to the original author(s) and the source, provide a link to the Creative Commons license and indicate if changes were made.

The images or other third party material in this chapter are included in the chapter's Creative Commons license, unless indicated otherwise in a credit line to the material. If material is not included in the chapter's Creative Commons license and your intended use is not permitted by statutory regulation or exceeds the permitted use, you will need to obtain permission directly from the copyright holder.

Chapter 4
One Rights: Indivisibility and Interdependence of Human and Animal Rights

> Those who are truly dedicated to human rights should not be afraid of characterizing their subject as a subset of a wider topic, that of animal rights. *Gearty (2009), p. 182.*

The previous chapters have argued that human rights can and should be extended to animals. This final part advocates the recognition of animal rights as new human rights. Accepting animal rights as the next generation of (non)human rights would constitute a seismic shift and likely lead to the formation of a new (post-)human rights paradigm.[1] Based on the indivisibility and interdependence of human and animal rights, this chapter proposes One Rights as a novel, holistic human rights paradigm for the Anthropocene.

4.1 Synthesis: Naturalistic and Political Justifications of Human and Animal Rights

The philosophical landscape of human rights features a great diversity of naturalistic and political approaches that put forth different foundational and practical justifications—and highlight various facets and functions—of human rights. Naturalistic conceptions are primarily concerned with the conceptual nature of human rights, the natural qualities of their holders, and the individual goods that rights protect. By contrast, political conceptions are primarily interested not in what human rights *are*, but in what human rights *do*.[2] This functionalism adds a useful analytical

---

[1] cf. Pietrzykowski (2020), p. 249 (noting that the 'idea of animal rights may actually become one of the most important and profound shifts in the paradigm of philosophical underpinnings of the law').

[2] See, critically, Tasioulas (2012), p. 6, 18 (arguing that human rights' functional role is ancillary to their conceptual nature. 'One can adequately grasp what a human right is without reference to any political role, just as one can understand what a nuclear weapon is without reference to its political uses').

layer for understanding and contextualizing the historicity, dynamism, and practical importance of human rights.

This book adopted a *pluralistic justificatory approach* to human and animal rights, reflective of their 'heterogeneous conceptual pedigree'.[3] It reviewed a wide range of naturalistic and political conceptions of human rights with regard to the animal question. A cross-cutting theme running through nearly all approaches is the explicit or implicit humanist tenet that human rights are believed to be rights of *humans*. Naturalistic conceptions arrive at this foundational justificatory nexus between human rights and humanity through different philosophical avenues, each identifying some aspect of (*unique* or *typical*) human nature as the rights-grounding feature. While human rights may appear definitionally exclusive of animals from the outset, a closer look revealed nuances of exclusivity across the spectrum of naturalistic theories, which yields more or less space for fitting animals into the human rights framework.[4] This book distinguished two families of (*exceptionalist* and *non-exceptionalist*) naturalistic theories that differ in terms of their commitment or agnosticism towards the idea of *human exceptionalism* and, consequently, in terms of the *programmatic* or *incidental* nature of exclusivity. The first, more senior strand of naturalistic thinking is informed by old humanism and marked by a belief in human exceptionalism. The demarcation from and exclusion of animals is inscribed into the very fabric of exceptionalist accounts, because they rely on a conception of special human nature that stylizes human uniqueness. The second, more junior family of naturalistic theories expresses a new humanism that is indifferent to human exceptionalism. These non-exceptionalist accounts are only incidentally exclusive but potentially inclusive of—indeed conceptually necessarily open to— animals, because they rest on a more realist or materialist conception of typical human nature that is cognizant of humans' animal nature and natural commonalities with other animals. Overall, the conceptual analysis has demonstrated that naturalistic theories of human rights are not homogenous in their exclusion of animals. Rather, exclusivity can be traced back to one particular strand of human rights theory that rests on an empirically unfounded belief in human exceptionalism, whereas a host of newer human rights conceptions are (perhaps) accidentally yet inherently inclusive of animals.

Political conceptions seek to emancipate human rights from human nature altogether, and instead give practical reasons for instituting human rights protections. This book has examined a range of practical reasons for extending human rights to animals, arguing that human rights are good for animals (the *principled argument*) and that animal rights are good for humans (the *prudential argument*). The prudential argument responds to the prevailing *antagonistic intuition*, which assumes that animal rights will be bad for human rights and subscribes to the (erroneous) belief that withholding rights from animals will serve to safeguard human rights. Whereas

---

[3] Hoffmann (2006), p. 405.

[4] See also Peters (2021b), p. 468 (concluding that 'the human rights model holds some promise for animal rights, but its "fit" to animals depends on the moral justifications espoused for those rights').

exceptionalist naturalistic accounts are conceptually invested in the ideology of human exceptionalism and in excluding animals, the antagonistic assumption reasserts human exceptionalism and exclusivity for practical reasons. Yet, as this book has argued, the antagonistic assumption is mistaken. In fact, the toxic ideology of human exceptionalism works to undermine rather than save human rights. Disrespecting animal rights is more likely to harm human rights, and respect for animal rights is more likely to benefit human rights. Accordingly, this book advanced a *synergistic understanding* of human and animal rights as mutually reinforcing and interdependent normative projects, for both *socio-political* and *eco-prudential* reasons. Humans and animals do not only share a similar human rights-generative experiential basis, but many forms of social injustice against humans and animals are further interconnected. Moreover, some of the gravest environmental human rights threats of our times are directly linked to our exploitation and extermination of animals. Integrating animal rights into the human rights mandate and protecting human and animal rights in tandem therefore appears to be the functionally better normative response to the human rights-relevant problems of discrimination, oppression, violence, dehumanization, as well as existential environmental and public health threats. While this book has placed much emphasis on the prudential (human-centric) argument, this is not to say that animal rights should be recognized purely or primarily for instrumental (anthropocentric or ecological) reasons. As the Ecuadorian Constitutional Court has recently reminded us, 'animals should not be protected only from an ecosystemic perspective or with a view to the needs of human beings, but mainly from a perspective that focuses on their individuality and intrinsic value.'[5] Such is the naturalistic and justice-based case for animal rights: because and to the extent that nonhuman animals—as sentient, suffering, vulnerable, oppressed, exploited, and kindred beings—share the relevant human rights-generative features (be they natural qualities or experiences of social injustice), human and animal rights can be grounded in common justifications (be they naturalistic or political).

In conclusion, the in-depth analysis of naturalistic and political conceptions suggests that human rights and animal rights are not only conceptually related, but also practically interdependent, synergistic, and mutually beneficial. Notwithstanding their *original humanism*, human rights need not—indeed cannot and should not—be understood as an exclusive (human exceptionalist), but rather, as an inclusive (transspecies universalist) normative paradigm that is amenable to an extension across the species barrier. Indeed, a common theme emerging from the review of contemporary human rights philosophy is that the evolving notion of human rights implicitly yet increasingly moves towards the inclusion of animal rights. While animals may not as yet be on the radar of most human rights theorists, and not on the map of human rights law, the inner logic of human rights (both as regards the conceptual structure and political function) has an inherent potential to integrate and

---

[5] Corte Constitucional del Ecuador, Final Judgment No. 253-20-JH/22 ('Estrellita Monkey' case) of 27 January 2022, para 79.

protect animals as well. The only hard exclusionary moment is found in old humanism of the exceptionalist and antagonistic variant, which is increasingly anachronistic and problematic with regard to its excluding and harmful effects not just on animals, but also on humans. Human rights proponents would be well-advised to dispense with human exceptionalism as their ideological basis and to take animal rights seriously, if not for principled then certainly for prudential reasons.

Consequently, this book concludes that human rights can and should be extended to animals, and that animal rights ought to be recognized as new human rights. But what would follow from the acceptance of animals as the newest members of the human rights family?

4.2 Human and Animal Rights as One Rights

4.2.1 Defining One Rights

Recognizing animal rights as new human rights means that human and animal rights become part of the same family of fundamental rights—expressed here as 'One Rights'. On this holistic understanding, human and animal rights are not simply independent instantiations of fundamental rights, but rather, kindred, indivisible, and interdependent rights.

The One Rights approach is a normative complement to the holistic One Health and One Welfare approaches. The One Health concept highlights that fundamentally 'health means the same for non-human animals as it does for humans', and One Welfare emphasizes that 'the concept of welfare is identical when applied to humans or to non-human animals'.[6] Moreover, both approaches acknowledge the interconnectedness and interdependence of human, animal, and environmental health and welfare.[7] Along similar lines, the One Rights approach has a conceptual and practical dimension. It is meant to assert that fundamentally, the *concept* of fundamental (or 'human') rights has the same core meaning as applied to humans and animals, and moreover, that these rights of humans and animals are *practically* interdependent.

The One Rights approach, so understood, is the logical conclusion of the analysis presented in this book. As regards the conceptual dimension of One Rights, the review of naturalistic justifications has highlighted the *conceptual indivisibility* of human and animal rights. Fundamental rights of *all* humans cannot consistently be theorized without simultaneously providing fertile grounds for animal rights to grow on. As Paola Cavalieri puts it: on the very basis that establishes them, human rights are not human. This is because the same justificatory arguments underlying human

---

[6] Broom and Johnson (2019), p. 3.
[7] See e.g. Amuasi et al. (2020), p. 1469.

rights also drive us towards attributing rights to animals.[8] Vice versa, Tom Regan asserts that the 'theory that rationally grounds the rights of animals also grounds the rights of humans.'[9] In terms of their conceptual nature, human and animal rights are essentially the same kind of rights, grounded in the same justifications.[10]

With regard to the practical dimension of One Rights, the review of political justifications has highlighted the *practical interdependence* of human and animal rights. Humans and animals—being part of the same planetary community, sharing many of the same environments, and often living in the same societies and political communities—are naturally and socially interdependent. It seems reasonable to think of human and animal rights, as normative protections of the natural and social preconditions for the enjoyment of rights, as equally interdependent. One Rights is sensitive to the socio-political and ecological interconnectedness of human and animal rights. In this vein—and set against the real-life backdrop of the Covid-19 pandemic and environmental crises—the Islamabad High Court recognized that animal rights have 'a nexus with the threat to human existence' and are an integral part of the human right to life, and thus affirmed the fundamental interdependence of human and animal rights.[11]

Simply put, One Rights means that human rights are animal rights and animal rights are human rights. However, as the following will show, this simplified formula requires more nuance: *some old* human rights are animal rights and animal rights are a *new generation* of human rights. It is further complicated by the ambiguous and evolving terminology of 'human rights': in actuality, human rights are human and nonhuman animal rights, and animal rights in this broad sense are post-human rights.

4.2.2 *(Some) Human Rights Are Animal Rights...*

Costas Douzinas notes that once we question 'the self-evidence of common sense, the intellectual reasons for creating human rights instead of rights for all living

---

[8] Cavalieri (2001), p. 139.
[9] Regan (1985), p. 24.
[10] See also Cochrane (2013), p. 672 (noting that 'human rights and the basic rights of other sentient creatures are not different in kind').
[11] Islamabad High Court 21 May 2020, W.P. No.1155/2019, paras 3, 55–57 (deliberating animal rights alongside, and as integral part of, human rights and environmental protection. The Court notes that the existence and survival of the human species is dependent on other living beings, and that it 'is, therefore, obvious that neglect of the welfare, wellbeing of the animal species, or any treatment of an animal that subjects it to unnecessary pain or suffering, has implications for the right to life of humans'. The Court further notes the link between violence against, and empathy for, humans and animals. In light of this, the Court concludes that any violations of animal rights also constitutes an 'infringement of the right to life of humans'); for a discussion, see Stucki and Sparks (2020).

beings are not clear.'[12] One Rights marks a clear departure from the terminologically reinforced truism that human rights are (exclusively) *human*, and submits that some human rights *are* animal rights. That is, some of the fundamental rights that humans have are the same kind of fundamental rights that animals (ought to) have, in virtue of their shared rights-generative properties. In terms of the specification of animal rights, there is a range of existing (civil, political, and social) human rights that may be extended and adapted to animals,[13] to the extent that animals display the prerequisite rights-generative interests, needs, vulnerabilities, or experiences of injustice. First and foremost, this includes the universal animal rights to life, bodily and mental integrity, liberty and freedom of movement, social and family life, freedom from slavery or involuntary servitude, and freedom from torture,[14] cruel, or inhumane treatment.[15] Furthermore, certain human rights may be extended to animals not because animals have an intrinsic interest in them, but because such instrumental rights function to better protect animals' fundamental interests. This includes the right to legal personhood (the right to have rights),[16] procedural rights such as the right to *habeas corpus* and access to justice, and possibly also some political rights ensuring that animals' interests receive adequate political representation and consideration.[17]

Recognizing animal rights as part of the human rights family does not mean that animals have all the same rights as humans, nor that all animals have the same rights as other animals.[18] First, conceptual continuity certainly does not imply that human and animal rights are coextensive. Rather, animals' rights must be differentiated in correspondence with animals' specific capacities, interests, and (functional) needs.[19] This means that many human rights are *not* animal rights, as animals do not need many of the rights that humans have, such as the right to freedom of religion or marriage.[20] It further means that animals may need some additional, 'zoo-specific' rights that differ from humans' rights, such as the 'fundamental right to be born, to

---

[12] Douzinas (2000), p. 184.

[13] See generally Stucki and Kurki (2020).

[14] See e.g. Gardner (2008), p. 4f (noting that 'the right not to be tortured may not be a human right. It is certainly true that all humans have this right, but arguably not only humans have it. If non-human animals have any rights at all, they have the right not to be tortured').

[15] See e.g. Donaldson and Kymlicka (2011), p. 49 (recognizing as core animal rights 'a range of universal negative rights—the right not to be tortured, experimented on, owned, enslaved, imprisoned, or killed').

[16] See e.g. Wise (2010).

[17] See e.g. Donaldson and Kymlicka (2011); Cochrane (2020).

[18] See also Schulz and Raman (2020), p. 164f; Sunstein (2003), p. 401 (noting that the 'legal protection to be accorded to animals does, of course, depend on the kind of creatures that they are ... the rights that animals deserve should be related to their capacities').

[19] See Beauchamp (2011), p. 204; Cochrane (2013), p. 665 ff.

[20] See also Abbey (2017), p. 6 (noting that 'no animal rights theorist says that all animals should enjoy all the same rights that humans should').

4.2 Human and Animal Rights as One Rights

live, grow and die in the proper environment for their species.'[21] Moreover, just as women, children, and persons with disabilities have a range of specific human rights,[22] certain animals may have some specific group-based or relational rights that other animals do not have, depending on their natural constitutions and social contexts. For example, domesticated animals, who have been bred, utilized, and made dependent on humans for centuries, should be accorded certain relational positive rights such as a right to health care, food, adequate living, and shelter.[23] Wild animals may require the right not to be domesticated and removed from their natural habitats[24] or collective sovereignty rights. Furthermore, animals who continue to perform services for humans may acquire (non-exploitative) labour rights.[25]

Overall, One Rights thus encompasses a normative continuum of *shared* and *differentiated* fundamental human and animal rights.

4.2.3 ... and (Human and Nonhuman) Animal Rights Are (Post-)Human Rights

To be sure, recognizing animal rights as the next generation of (non)human rights will send 'discursive irritations' or 'shockwaves'[26] through the human rights universe—but such was and is generally the nature of old rights revolutions and new human rights evolution. Historically, fundamental rights were enjoyed by *some* (free adult male) humans, but not by women, children, or (formerly) enslaved people.[27] It took several rights revolutions for human rights to be extended to *all* humans. Since the early formulations of the rights of *man*, human rights evolution has been characterized by a 'moral extensionism'[28] and a 'widening of the circle of

---

[21] Tercer Juzgado de Garantías de Mendoza 3 November 2016, Expte Nro P-72.254/15 (further noting that recognizing fundamental animal rights 'is not about granting them the same rights humans have'); Peters (2021b), p. 469 (arguing that it 'seems best to stop analogical thinking and design animal rights as animal rights, with their zoo-specific rationale and telos').

[22] Convention on the Elimination of All Forms of Discrimination against Women (1979); Convention on the Rights of the Child (1989); Convention on the Rights of Persons with Disabilities (2006).

[23] See generally Donaldson and Kymlicka (2011) (distinguishing different types of relational rights for domesticated, wild, and liminal animals).

[24] Corte Constitucional del Ecuador, Final Judgment No. 253-20-JH/22 ('Estrellita Monkey' case) of 27 January 2022, para 111ff.

[25] See e.g. Cochrane (2023); Blattner et al. (2019).

[26] Hoffmann (2006), p. 409.

[27] See also Peters (2021a), p. 14f (noting the 'contradiction between the universalist language and the exclusivity of rights holders' of early human rights, which were reserved for the 'privileged happy few').

[28] Vincent (2010), p. 146.

rights holders'[29]—a gradual process of extending rights to formerly excluded groups. Today, some say the human rights 'balloon' is fully expanded or even overstretched, but surely those (nonhumans) who remain right-less would beg to differ.[30] As Conor Gearty submits, there is no reason in principle why the 'outward momentum' of human rights should be 'permanently blocked at a species barrier'.[31] Just as *old* human rights have been formed in reaction to historical experiences of injustice and specific political threats to humans, *new* human rights continue to emerge as new (or entrenched) forms of injustice become more widely recognized or as novel threats to old human rights appear. Both these conditions for human rights (r)evolution are present with regard to animal rights: a growing awareness of animal injustice and the intersecting oppression of humans and animals, as well as an increasing interdependence of humans and animals in the face of new existential risks arising in the Anthropocene.

Extending human rights to animals would certainly mark a (non)human rights revolution, though in some respects, this may be less revolutionary than it appears. For one thing, (human) animals already have human rights, and in this trivial sense, human rights are naturally animal rights. Furthermore, in a legal sense, the human rights universe is already populated by nonhuman right-holders, notably corporations, which are entitled to (some) international and constitutional human rights protections.[32] In a philosophical sense, recognizing nonhuman animals as a new class of right-holders is but a progressing continuation of the natural rights and human rights tradition.[33] But in a more profound sense, the nonhuman rights revolution has paradigm-shifting implications for the concept of human rights.[34] It marks an 'animal turn' or 'posthuman turn' in human rights, after which human rights are no longer human, but more-than-human rights—they are (human and nonhuman) animal rights.

On a conceptual level, One Rights generally and fundamentally means that *human rights are not (just) human rights at all*. Rather, we need to rethink the

---

[29] D'Amato and Chopra (1991), p. 51.

[30] See Peters (2021a), p. 8.

[31] Gearty (2009), p. 182; D'Amato and Chopra (1991), p. 51 (noting that against the historical backdrop of a widening circle of rights-holders, 'there is nothing strange about recognizing the rights of whales – creatures that are more animate than corporations, more communicative than infants and mentally enfeebled persons, more communal than the society of nations, and perhaps more intelligent than the smartest human beings'); Singer (2011), p. 124 (arguing that 'if ethics grows to take into account the interests of all sentient creatures, the expansion of our moral horizons will at last have completed its long and erratic course').

[32] See e.g. van den Muijsenbergh and Rezai (2012); Isiksel (2016, 2019); Khoury and Whyte (2021).

[33] See e.g. Goodkin (1987), p. 268 (the 'recognition of animal rights is the logical progression in the continued evolution of natural law/natural rights theories'); Donaldson and Kymlicka (2011), p. 44 ('animal rights as a logical extension of the doctrine of human rights'); Cavalieri (2001), p. 143 (the extension of human rights to animals as 'necessary dialectical derivation of ... human rights theory').

[34] On the paradigm-shifting sense of normative revolutions, see Peters (2015), p. 25f.

concept of human rights as a larger category of (human and nonhuman) animal rights, and actual *human* rights as a subset of animal rights. Accordingly, the term 'human rights' becomes a misnomer, and we may need to 'recast the nomenclature of "human" rights'.[35] Just as the historically antecedent 'rights of man' have been replaced by the more (women-)inclusive term 'human rights',[36] perhaps the phrase 'human rights' should now be retired to make way for a more (animal-)inclusive notion of (human and nonhuman) animal rights.[37] What results from the deconstruction of human rights, then, is not their destruction, but their reconstruction as a wider set of human and nonhuman animal rights. In this sense, human rights turned into (human and nonhuman) animal rights are *post-human rights*—not 'rights of posthumans', nor an anti-humanist regression, but rather, a post-humanist progression of human rights.

4.3 One Rights as Holistic (Post-)Human Rights Paradigm for the Anthropocene

What this book set out to do was the deconstruction of (old) human rights and their reconstruction as (human and nonhuman) animal rights under a holistic One Rights paradigm. The themes of this book are part of a larger conversation about shifting legal paradigms, and emerging post-humanist paradigms, in the Anthropocene.[38] Law is traditionally and unapologetically configured as an 'essentially human institution'.[39] It is a decisively 'anthropocentric institution' that is not only made by and enacted through humans, but also centres on the (rational) human as its (main) legal subject and entrenches the primacy of human interests over virtually all other concerns.[40] This old 'juridical humanism'—expressive of anthropocentrism and human exceptionalism—belongs to the hallmarks of Western legal culture, but

---

[35] Vincent (2010), p. 147.

[36] On the shift in terminology, see Hunt (2007), p. 22ff.

[37] See Edmundson (2012), p. 158; D'Amato and Chopra (1991), p. 27 (noting that 'the phrase "human rights" is only superficially species chauvinistic. In a profound sense, whales and some other sentient mammals are entitled to human rights or at least to *humanist rights* – to the most fundamental entitlements that we regard as part of the humanitarian tradition'); Cochrane (2013), p. 659, proposes the term 'sentient rights' and submits that human and animal rights are part of a 'shared scheme of "sentient rights"'; Fasel (2019), p. 158, proposes the term 'fundamental rights' to describe both human and animal rights.

[38] See e.g. Deckha (2021).

[39] Pietrzykowski (2020), p. 249.

[40] Deckha (2013), p. 784, 813; see also Corte Constitucional del Ecuador, Final Judgment No. 253-20-JH/22 ('Estrellita Monkey' case) of 27 January 2022, para 75 (noting the 'marked anthropocentrism' of modern law, whereby 'the human being has been considered the center of all legal expression').

is increasingly seen as problematic and anachronistic.[41] The growing discontent with traditional humanism is fuelled by the insight that 'Anthropocentrism is inextricably connected to the rise of the Anthropocene'.[42] Enabled by a permissive legal system, unrestrained human dominance over the natural world has grown into a full-blown planetary crisis. Perhaps the 'silver lining to the onset of the Anthropocene' is that it has opened up the 'discursive space' necessary for critically re-examining and reconfiguring the law.[43]

Francesca Ferrando submits that posthumanism (in the sense of *post-anthropocentrism*)[44] is 'the philosophy of our time' and the philosophical approach that best suits the 'geological time of the Anthropocene'.[45] Indeed, in order to resolve the monumental problems that have been facilitated by *anthropocentric humanism*, it seems warranted to foster normative paradigms of a *post-humanist, post-anthropocentric* nature. Posthumanism proposes a 'new way of understanding the human subject in relationship to the natural world',[46] one that abandons or softens 'the idea that humans are a superior species in the natural order.'[47] Whereas anthropocentrism postulates the 'centrality and privileged position of humanity vis-à-vis the rest of the world',[48] post-anthropocentrism asks us to decentre the human and to consider 'the pluralistic symphony' of human and nonhuman voices that have been silenced and excluded by old humanism.[49]

Human rights is one such paradigm that needs to be modernized to better fit the new reality and challenges of the Anthropocene. Posthumanist ideas have already infiltrated into human rights discourse.[50] Efforts to rethink the traditionally humanist institution of human rights through a post-anthropocentric lens range from

---

[41] Pietrzykowski (2020), p. 249 et passim; see also Koskenniemi (2020), p. 424 (noting that 'No myth has enchanted modern lawyers more deeply than the Promethean one about humans taking nature for their use. It is time to let go of that myth').

[42] Ferrando (2019), p. 103f; see also Lewis and Maslin (2015), p. 178 (noting that 'More widespread recognition that human actions are driving far-reaching changes to the life-supporting infrastructure of Earth may well have increasing philosophical, social, economic and political implications').

[43] Gellers (2021), p. 1.

[44] While 'posthumanism' is an umbrella term that covers a variety of philosophical movements—including variants of trans-, post- and antihumanism (see Ferrando (2013), p. 26)—it is here taken to indicate a rejection of traditional humanism—which is by definition anthropocentric—and thus understood as 'post-anthropocentrism'. See generally Bolter (2016), p. 1; Ferrando (2019), p. 24 ('Posthumanism is a "post" to the notion of the "human," located within the historical occurrence of "humanism" ... and in an uncritical acceptance of "anthropocentrism"'); Wolfe (2010), p. xv (noting that posthumanism 'is only posthuman*ist*, in the sense that it opposes the fantasies of disembodiment and autonomy, inherited from humanism itself').

[45] Ferrando (2019), p. 1, 22.

[46] Bolter (2016), p. 1.

[47] Miah (2008), p. 72.

[48] Kotzé and Villavicencio Calzadilla (2017), p. 402f.

[49] Ferrando (2019), p. 103.

[50] See e.g. Baxi (2009), p. 197ff; Grear (2018).

'greening' old human rights (what might be called 'environmental human rights law')[51] to recognizing rights of nature, which may be considered the 'epitome' of non-anthropocentric rights approaches.[52] Animal rights, too, fall squarely into this category of post-humanist rights that seek to overcome the 'anthropocentricity of "human" rights as such.'[53] Although human rights—and law at large—will realistically always retain a certain degree of anthropocentrism, Catherine Redgwell notes that traditional humanism is being displaced by a 'dilute anthropocentrism' that recognizes the 'interrelatedness and interdependence of the natural world of which human beings form a part.'[54] This book has tentatively furnished a post-humanist, post-anthropocentric, post-human rights paradigm—one that emancipates human rights from its exceptionalist foundations, includes nonhumans, and is sensitive to the interdependence of humans, animals, and their shared environment. And while beyond the scope of this book, the One Rights approach could (and perhaps should) also accommodate the rights of nature.[55] Indeed, integrating human, animal, and nature rights under a holistic One Rights framework might be considered the next logical step, and may be an important topic for future research.

Jack Donnelly notes that human rights 'ultimately rest on a social decision to act as if such "things" existed—and then, through social action directed by these rights, to make real the world that they envision.'[56] We, as a society and global community, have long decided to treat human rights as exclusive things, created by and for humans. Yet, our commitment to human exceptionalism has forged a real world that is inhospitable to many marginalized humans, and will likely become inhabitable for large portions of humanity unless we embark on a 'dramatic change of direction'.[57] For human rights—and humanity—to survive in the Anthropocene, we need to let go of traditional human rights exceptionalism or 'supremacism'.[58] As this book has sought to show, embracing a more inclusive version of (post-)human rights as (interdependent human and nonhuman) animal rights promises to achieve better rights-protective outcomes for humans, animals, and their shared planetary home. Indeed, One Rights may help us link up into a true 'planetary community',[59] governed by a post-anthropocentric human rights culture.

---

[51] See Knox (2021), p. 785.

[52] See Handl (2020), p. 148.

[53] von Arnauld et al. (2020), p. 3; see also Schweitzer (2021), p. 29f (noting that 'law itself seems to be increasingly turning against its anthropocentric foundation as more and more court rulings recognize the legal personhood of animals' and that animal rights 'may appear as a posthumanist approach to law in that they are capable of decentering "the human"').

[54] Redgwell (1996), p. 73 (further noting that this 'Weak anthropocentrism is less hierarchical and does not perceive the non-human world solely as a means to a human ends').

[55] On rights of nature, see generally Boyd (2017); Kotzé and Villavicencio Calzadilla (2017); Houck (2017).

[56] Donnelly (2013), p. 22.

[57] Boyd (2019), p. 20.

[58] Kymlicka (2018).

[59] Rabossi (1990), p. 162; Rorty (1993), p. 125.

References

Abbey R (2017) Closer Kinships: Rortyan resources for animal rights. Contemp Polit Theory 16:1–18
Amuasi JH, Lucas T, Horton R, Winkler AS (2020) Reconnecting for our future: the lancet one health commission. The Lancet 395:1469–1471
Baxi U (2009) Human rights in a posthuman world. Oxford University Press, Oxford
Beauchamp TL (2011) Rights theory and animal rights. In: Beauchamp TL, Frey RG (eds) Oxford handbook of animal ethics. Oxford University Press, Oxford, pp 198–227
Blattner CE, Coulter K, Kymlicka W (eds) (2019) Animal labour: a new frontier of interspecies justice? Oxford University Press, Oxford
Bolter JD (2016) Posthumanism. In: Jensen KB, Rothenbuhler EW, Pooley JD, Craig RT (eds) The International Encyclopedia of Communication Theory and Philosophy. Wiley Blackwell. https://doi.org/10.1002/9781118766804.wbiect220
Boyd DR (2017) The rights of nature: a legal revolution that could save the world. ECW Press, Toronto
Boyd DR (2019) Human rights obligations relating to the enjoyment of a safe, clean, healthy and sustainable environment: Report of the Special Rapporteur on Human Rights and the Environment. 19 July 2019, A/74/161
Broom DM, Johnson KG (2019) Stress and animal welfare: key issues in the biology of humans and other animals, 2nd edn. Springer, Cham
Cavalieri P (2001) The animal question: why nonhuman animals deserve human rights. Oxford University Press, Oxford
Cochrane A (2013) From human rights to sentient rights. Crit Rev Int Soc Polit Philosophy 16:655–675
Cochrane A (2020) Should animals have political rights? Polity Press, Cambridge
Cochrane A (2023) Animals as labourers. In: Peters A, Stilt K, Stucki S (eds) Oxford handbook of global animal law. Oxford University Press, Oxford (forthcoming)
D'Amato A, Chopra SK (1991) Whales: their emerging right to life. Am J Int Law 85:21–62
Deckha M (2013) Initiating a non-anthropocentric jurisprudence: the rule of law and animal vulnerability under a property paradigm. Alberta Law Rev 50:783–814
Deckha M (2021) Animals as legal beings: contesting anthropocentric legal orders. University of Toronto Press, Toronto
Donaldson S, Kymlicka W (2011) Zoopolis: A political theory of animal rights. Oxford University Press, Oxford
Donnelly J (2013) Universal human rights in theory and practice, 3rd edn. Cornell University Press, Ithaca
Douzinas C (2000) The end of human rights: critical legal thought at the turn of the century. Hart, Oxford
Edmundson WA (2012) An introduction to rights, 2nd edn. Cambridge University Press, Cambridge
Fasel RN (2019) More equal than others: animals in the age of human rights aristocracy, PhD thesis. University of Cambridge
Ferrando F (2013) Posthumanism, transhumanism, antihumanism, metahumanism, and new materialisms. Existenz 8(2):26–32
Ferrando F (2019) Philosophical posthumanism. Bloomsbury, London
Gardner J (2008) 'Simply in Virtue of Being Human': the whos and whys of human rights. J Ethics Soc Philosophy 2(2):1–23. https://doi.org/10.26556/jesp.v2i2.23
Gearty C (2009) Is human rights speciesist? In: Linzey A (ed) The link between animal abuse and human violence. Sussex Academic Press, Brighton, pp 175–183
Gellers JC (2021) Earth system law and the legal status of non-humans in the anthropocene. Earth System Governance 7:100083
Goodkin SL (1987) The evolution of animal rights. Columbia Human Rights Law Rev 18:259–288

References

Grear A (2018) Human rights and new horizons? Thoughts toward a new juridical ontology. Sci Technol Human Values 43:129–145

Handl G (2020) The human right to a clean environment and rights of nature: between advocacy and reality. In: von Arnauld A, von der Decken K, Susi M (eds) Cambridge handbook of new human rights: recognition, novelty, rhetoric. Cambridge University Press, Cambridge, pp 137–153

Hoffmann FF (2006) 'Shooting into the Dark': toward a pragmatic theory of human rights (activism). Texas Int Law J 41:403–414

Houck OA (2017) Noah's second voyage: the rights of nature as law. Tulane Environ Law J 31:1–50

Hunt L (2007) Inventing human rights: a history. W.W. Norton & Company, New York/London

Isiksel T (2016) The rights of man and the rights of the man-made: corporations and human rights. Human Rights Q 38:294–349

Isiksel T (2019) Corporate human rights claims under the ECHR. Georgetown J Law Public Policy 17:979–1005

Khoury S, Whyte D (2021) Human rights for profit: the system-preserving tendencies of the regional human rights courts. Capital Class 46:189–209

Knox JH (2021) Human rights. In: Rajamani L, Peel J (eds) Oxford handbook of international environmental law, 2nd edn. Oxford University Press, Oxford, pp 784–799

Koskenniemi M (2020) Enchanted by the tools? An enlightenment perspective. Am Univ Int Law Rev 35:397–426

Kotzé L, Villavicencio Calzadilla P (2017) Somewhere between rhetoric and reality: environmental constitutionalism and the rights of nature in Ecuador. Transnatl Environ Law 6:401–433

Kymlicka W (2018) Human rights without human supremacism. Canadian J Philosophy 48:763–792

Lewis SL, Maslin MA (2015) Defining the anthropocene. Nature 519:171–180

Miah A (2008) A critical history of posthumanism. In: Gordijn B, Chadwick R (eds) Medical enhancement and posthumanity. Springer, Heidelberg, pp 71–94

Peters A (2015) Introduction: animal law – a paradigm change. In: Peters A, Stucki S, Boscardin L (eds) Animal law: reform or revolution? Schulthess, Zürich, pp 15–30

Peters A (2021a) The importance of having rights. Heidelberg J Int Law 81:7–22

Peters A (2021b) Animals in international law. Pocketbooks of the Hague academy of international law. Brill/Nijhoff, Leiden

Pietrzykowski T (2020) Animal rights. In: von Arnauld A, von der Decken K, Susi M (eds) Cambridge handbook of new human rights: recognition, novelty, rhetoric. Cambridge University Press, Cambridge, pp 243–252

Rabossi E (1990) La Teoria de los Derechos Humanos Naturalizada. Revista del Centro de Estudios Constitucionales 5:159–175

Redgwell C (1996) Life, the universe and everything: a critique of anthropocentric rights. In: Boyle AE, Anderson MR (eds) Human rights approaches to environmental protection. Clarendon Press, Oxford, pp 71–87

Regan T (1985) The case for animal rights. In: Singer P (ed) In defense of animals. Basil Blackwell, New York, pp 13–26

Rorty R (1993) Human rights, rationality, and sentimentality. In: Shute S, Hurley S (eds) On human rights: the Oxford Amnesty Lectures. Basic Books, New York, pp 111–134

Schulz WF, Raman S (2020) The coming good society: why new realities demand new rights. Harvard University Press, Cambridge

Schweitzer D (2021) 'Rights of Things': A posthumanist approach to law? Nat Cult 16:28–46

Singer P (2011) The expanding circle: ethics, evolution, and moral progress (with a new preface and afterword). Princeton University Press, Princeton

Stucki S, Kurki V (2020) Animal rights. In: Sellers M, Kirste S (eds) Encyclopedia of the philosophy of law and social philosophy. Springer, Dordrecht. https://doi.org/10.1007/978-94-007-6730-0_407-1

Stucki S, Sparks T (2020) The Elephant in the (Court)Room: Interdependence of Human and Animal Rights in the Anthropocene. EJIL:Talk, 9 June 2020. https://www.ejiltalk.org/the-elephant-in-the-courtroom-interdependence-of-human-and-animal-rights-in-the-anthropocene/

Sunstein CR (2003) The rights of animals. Univ Chicago Law Rev 70:387–401

Tasioulas J (2012) Towards a philosophy of human rights. Curr Legal Probl 65:1–30

van den Muijsenbergh WHAM, Rezai S (2012) Corporations and the European Convention on Human Rights. Glob Bus Dev Law J 25:43–68

Vincent A (2010) The politics of human rights. Oxford University Press, Oxford

von Arnauld A, von der Decken K, Susi M (2020) Introduction. In: von Arnauld A, von der Decken K, Susi M (eds) Cambridge handbook of new human rights: recognition, novelty, rhetoric. Cambridge University Press, Cambridge, pp 1–4

Wise SM (2010) Legal personhood and the nonhuman rights project. Anim Law Rev 17:1–12

Wolfe C (2010) What is posthumanism? University of Minnesota Press, Minneapolis

Open Access This chapter is licensed under the terms of the Creative Commons Attribution 4.0 International License (http://creativecommons.org/licenses/by/4.0/), which permits use, sharing, adaptation, distribution and reproduction in any medium or format, as long as you give appropriate credit to the original author(s) and the source, provide a link to the Creative Commons license and indicate if changes were made.

The images or other third party material in this chapter are included in the chapter's Creative Commons license, unless indicated otherwise in a credit line to the material. If material is not included in the chapter's Creative Commons license and your intended use is not permitted by statutory regulation or exceeds the permitted use, you will need to obtain permission directly from the copyright holder.

GPSR Compliance
The European Union's (EU) General Product Safety Regulation (GPSR) is a set of rules that requires consumer products to be safe and our obligations to ensure this.

If you have any concerns about our products, you can contact us on

ProductSafety@springernature.com

In case Publisher is established outside the EU, the EU authorized representative is:

Springer Nature Customer Service Center GmbH
Europaplatz 3
69115 Heidelberg, Germany